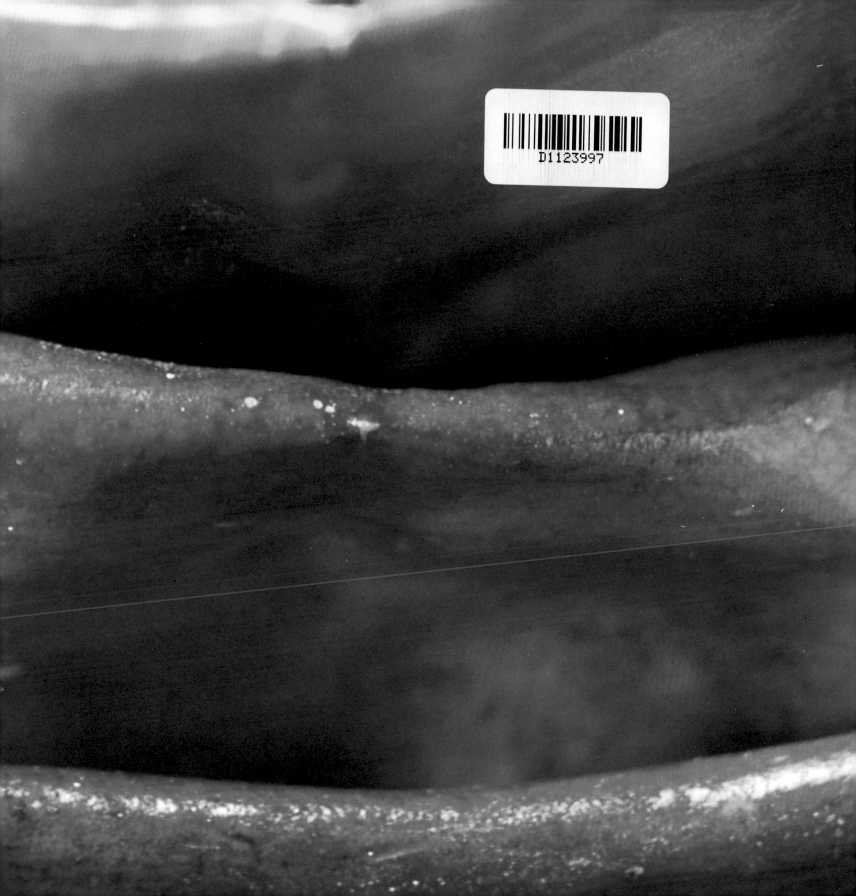

la porte des indes

COOKBOOK

Mehernosh and Sherin Mody

John Hellon

Photography by Tony le Duc

PAVILION

CONTENTS

preface

Since 1982 I have taken groups of curry enthusiasts on my 21-day Gourmet Tours to India. The highlight is a cooking demonstration by the Taj hotel group's Director of Cuisine, *Chef Culinaire* Satish Arora, India's most respected chef. Both Mehernosh Mody and his wife Sherin have come under his direction. For a lyrical hour Satish performs with panache, expertise and humour, all on his own except for the help of just one of his youngest rising stars. Back in 1986, for the first time he used a female assistant. It was Sherin and it was memorable.

When Mehernosh and Sherin came together in London a new magic was born. La Porte began quietly, taking some time to achieve its first full house. But this is the correct way to wean a new team in a huge new venue. Once the kitchen found its feet, Sherin took up the position of General Manager and this move gave the front of house a new strength.

Wearing my Cobra Good Curry Guide hat, it was already clear that this restaurant could not be bettered. Once it had gained confidence I was proud to award it the unique accolade of Best UK Restaurant, not once but twice – no mean feat when you consider that there are 8,500 Indian restaurants in Britain.

Wearing my chef's hat, I have had the privilege of working at La Porte on more than one occasion. The tiny kitchen comes as quite a shock to visitors and it requires intense discipline when producing food for 300 diners of the quality required by Mehernosh. But this is the way Mehernosh designed it and wants it. There are no egos in the kitchen; just quiet, hard-working professionalism from Mehernosh and his dedicated team and this is how it should be. And the food is as it should be too. It is accurately cooked, superb Indian regional food. Mehernosh encourages innovation but he does not allow it to lose touch with authentic Indian reality. In addition, he actively welcomes the opportunity to show off the team's expertise by regularly running food festivals and cookery demonstrations.

The next piece in the jigsaw was for Mehernosh to share his culinary secrets in the pages of a cookery book. This fine work has taken several years to metabolise. Cookery books are not easy to write. Recipes must be exciting and alluring enough to tempt the reader to try them. They must not be ambiguous, nor complex. Above all, they must work. I am delighted to say that La Porte des Indes Cookbook achieves all of these attributes. This comes as no surprise. It is such attention to detail which keeps La Porte in its top, world-class position.

PAT CHAPMAN
Founder of The Curry Club and Editor of the *Cobra Good Curry Guide*

the french connection

Why should an Indian restaurant in London have a French name?

The simple answer is that La Porte des Indes was born in an unequivocally French-speaking environment, an elegant *maison de maître* on Brussels' Avenue Louise. From the beginning in 1984, the restaurant set out to present authentic regional Indian cuisine of the highest quality in a luxuriant and evocative setting. Highly qualified and talented chefs were recruited from different regions of India and, in their wake, came antiques, craft objects and folk art to transform the Brussels mansion into a romantic microcosm of the sub-continent.

Indian cuisine is, of course, well known for its regional character. The *tandoor* oven, for example, originated in the North West. Only comparatively recently have those marinated and *tandoor*-baked fish, poultry and meat dishes spread to the rest of India and round the world. Bombay is known in particular for its splendid variety of street food, origin of a wealth of restaurant starters, as well as its sophisticated Parsee cuisine, unbound by religious food taboos.

Seafood and pork truly come into their own in Goa, together with the European influence of the Portuguese, who arrived in 1510 and who also, incidentally, introduced chillies from Latin America to the East. Perhaps rather less remembered, at least in Britain, is the arrival in 1670 on India's south-eastern coast of the French. There was even a moment when hegemony over a large part of the sub-continent hung in the balance between the two colonial powers. And the Pondicherry enclave was to last until 1954.

For almost 300 years, therefore, a Créole community of people of French extraction and of Franco-Indians lived there and, indeed, it survives to this day. Could not this conjunction of two great cuisine cultures have generated its own regional specialities? And, if so, have any survived almost half a century after the official departure of the French? Furthermore, could not the most interesting dishes with a French accent be added to the restaurant's already wide range of regional fare? And provide additional justification for a London branch of La Porte des Indes to retain its original name into the bargain?

Executive Chef Mehernosh Mody and his manager wife Sherin set off to investigate. To discover what they found, read on...

a tale of storm and stress

A POTTED HISTORY OF THE FRENCH IN INDIA

The French were not the first Europeans to drop anchor in the Bay of Bengal close to the site of modern Pondicherry, Pondichéry or Pondy for short. Amazingly the ancient Romans traded there, as witnessed by coins, pottery made in Arezzo and, handily for dating, an engraving of the head of Caesar Augustus. It took another millennium and a half before the then ubiquitous Portuguese set up a trading station around 1550. But this chapter, like many of those that follow, was brief.

There was a war of succession in the ruling kingship of Gingee (pronounced Shingee), now a deserted and almost forgotten complex of ruined forts some fifty miles to the northwest. Unluckily for the Portuguese, they backed the wrong horse. In 1617 the ruler of Gingee gave permission to a Frenchman, Jean Pépin, to set up in Pondy but, not for the last time, events in Europe – in this case the Thirty Years War – distracted France and instead the Danes traded there intermittently up to the 1650's. And Britain's East India Company established a trading post further up the coast at Madras, nearly twenty years before taking over Bombay.

In 1670, the Sultan of Bijapur, nominal ruler of the region, in turn invited the French to set up a

trading post. But local power remained in the hands of warlords and the crucial invitation came from one Shere Khan Lodi, governor of the fort of Ranjankudi, concerned by the arrogance of the Dutch, also trading along the coast. The negotiations were conducted on behalf of the *Compagnie des Indes Orientales* (French equivalent of the East India Company) by François Martin, the true creator of French Pondicherry.

Appointed Governor in 1675, he established Pondy on a firm commercial footing. Textiles were the mainstay of his products for trading which also included pearls and coral. Remarkably for a businessman of the time, he refused to traffic in slaves. *"Je le trouvai trop indigne pour une compagnie"* – I found it unworthy of a company – he wrote.

War between the French and the Dutch back in Europe resulted in Pondy being seized by the latter in 1693. Martin was imprisoned. But four years later, with hostilities ended, France was able to buy the territory back. Louis the Fourteenth created a Sovereign Council with the right to strike its own coinage in Pondy and Martin was re-appointed Governor.

Under his leadership the town grew in prosperity, while his talent for diplomacy enabled him to navigate the stormy seas of power struggles among the warlords. But further afield the mighty Mughal empire was crumbling, creating a dangerous power vacuum. Martin resolved to reinforce the protection of the town and, before his death at the age of 73 on the eve of the year 1707, Pondy was surrounded by redoubtable fortifications. It was going to need them.

The history of Pondy and, indeed, of France in India in the eighteenth century is a tale of what might have been. It's important to remember that both France and Britain, sworn enemies and by then the two significant European players, continued to be represented by two private companies whose objective was to reinforce their trading positions. With uncertain support from their home countries, both were riding the tigers of shaky alliances with equally

Vue de Pondichéry vers 1790

shaky rulers as the Hindu Marathas replaced the Mughals. They fought battles with armies of *sepoys* (recruits from the Indian population) led by officers of the two trading companies; on the French side Dupleix and on the British Clive, who came to be known as Clive of India.

Dupleix was appointed governor of Pondy in 1742. Four years later he captured Madras from the British, another echo of events in Europe where Britain had sided with the Austrians against the French in the War of the Austrian Succession. The British put Pondy to siege in their turn but Martin's fortifications proved their worth.

A few years later a brilliant young French officer, Bussy, supported by Dupleix, took the side of the pretender to the throne of the Nizam of Hyderabad. After a decisive battle, led by Bussy, the pretender won and the new Nizam heaped rewards on Dupleix, including territory. It was 1750 – Pondy's moment of glory when the French dominated over the British in India and seemed poised to create an empire. Just eleven years later there was nothing left.

In 1752 a coalition of the Rajah of Tanjore, the King of Mysore and Marathan led by Clive forced the French to retreat to the gates of Pondy. Two years later, after leading costly and fruitless counterattacks, Dupleix was recalled to France, the prosperity of Pondy in ruins.

Four years later, war broke out once again between the French and the British in Europe. In India, after a British victory near Bengal, the French appointed Lally Tollendal as Governor of Pondy. Tollendal, an Irish catholic and Jacobite, had emigrated to France where he nursed an insatiable hatred for the English. He launched a quixotic attack on Madras, which had been returned to the British in '49. Routed, he was pursued to Pondy, recalling Bussy in the process and thereby losing the allegiance of France's remaining Indian allies. The siege of Pondy lasted for one terrible year. When the British took the town in 1761 it was the end of the dream of a French empire that might have been. The postscript has an awful symmetry. The Governor of Madras, Lord Pigot, a French protestant Huguenot, who had emigrated to England, razed the French section of Pondicherry and expelled the inhabitants. Tollendal was returned to France where he was executed for high treason.

Pondy was returned to France in 1762 and was soon repopulated by the French. But it knew little peace and was besieged several times more before being retaken by the British. As its tumultuous century drew to a close, far away in Egypt Napoleon plotted with Tippu Sultan, arch enemy of the British, to drive them out of India. An expeditionary force even set sail from Toulon. But it was soon diverted to fulfil more pressing needs closer to home. Finally in 1816 what was left of Pondy was restored to France for the last time.

Neglected by France and harassed by Britain, the first half of the nineteenth century was a difficult time for Pondy. Nevertheless, the town that now looks so charmingly French was beginning to take shape with its fine white stuccoed public buildings, its library and its schools. This must have been partly funded by a dubious trade in indentured labourers, exported sometimes virtually under duress to Reunion, Mauritius and the Caribbean. One suspects that François Martin would not have approved. The practice ended in 1885.

In the second half of the century, steamships and the newly constructed Suez Canal brought growth and the return of prosperity. Come the twentieth century and the Second World War, and Pondy was the first French overseas territory to rally to General de Gaulle's call to arms. Some thousand young men joined the Free French forces.

Finally, on the first of November 1954, Pondy became part of India. Since then new industries have been developed and the population has more than doubled. The famous ashram, founded by Sri Aurobindo early in the century, and its offshoot in nearby Auroville with its international community dedicated to demonstrating that people of all cultures and races can live together in harmony, have indubitably contributed to the pristine condition of the city, which is probably the cleanest and best preserved on the sub-continent.

Pondy is very much an Indian city. Yet, with its Lycée, its Alliance Française, its policemen in their red kepis, its restaurants, its charming old colonial houses with their luxuriant gardens and the frequent sound of the French language being spoken by a cosmopolitan crowd, a little of its soul still belongs to France.

the story of la porte des indes

Once upon a time there was a ballroom. Long abandoned, it lay mouldering behind the sober façade of a London city street. Until one day it was re-discovered and transformed into a dream palace where relics of the old French territory of Pondicherry in the Bay of Bengal mingled with the art and architecture of the Mughal empire and other treasures from all over India. The transformation was part of the concept of Karl Steppe, founder of the Blue Elephant Group and an antiquarian specialising. It was made spectacular reality by Yves Burton, the Group's interior designer. However, the heart of a restaurant, beautiful as it may be, is located in its kitchen. Enter Sherin and Mehernosh Mody.

Both Sherin, General Manager, and Mehernosh, Executive Chef, were born in Mumbai. Her family hails from Kerala. His family is Parsee. Both families were pleased when their offspring enrolled at the Bombay Catering College. On leaving the college both of them were snapped up by India's most prestigious hotel group. It was the ideal apprenticeship. For seven years they travelled the length and breadth of the sub-continent as they both gained management skills

and knowledge of regional cuisines, given depth by the talented chefs they encountered. Later this was to stand them in good stead. Through their contacts, maintained over the years, the Modys were able to recruit a team of superb regional Indian chefs offering a gamut of authentic dishes unrivalled by any other restaurant in London.

But the story of La Porte des Indes did not begin in Britain's capital. The concept was born in a tall, turn-of-the-century house on the Avenue Louise in Brussels. It was first spotted by Nooror Somany, Karl Steppé's partner, a highly talented and inventive cook with a passion for Indian fare.

It took courage to decide to create an Indian restaurant in a country where the cuisine of the sub-continent was little known and even less appreciated. Undaunted, Nooror set out for India. She spent months working in the kitchens of one of Bombay's most distinguished establishments and travelling the land, meeting chefs and sampling the food of the regions, while Karl hunted for the antiques, objects and textiles that Yves Burton then deployed in his transformation of the house on the Avenue Louise. Finally, entering the house became like stumbling on a portal into a faraway, enchanting world. If ever a restaurant lived up to its name, it was the original Porte des Indes.

The arrival of the now Executive Chef, Rajesh Dalaya, was to mark a step in the evolution of the enterprise. Born in Poona, at seven Rajesh found himself in Calcutta. More moves followed, wherever his engineer father was posted; to Madras, Bombay, Benares, Hyderabad. And everywhere his mother, a keen cook, explored the regional cuisine. Shortly before he graduated in hotel management at the university of Calcutta he was recruited by India's most prestigious hotel group and, five years later had risen to head chef at one of the group's flagship restaurants. And it was in the kitchen that he first met Nooror, deep in her research of Indian regional cuisine. Years later she tracked him down in Saudi Arabia.

Mehernosh joined the Blue Elephant Group, and as the plans for London's Porte des Indes began to take shape, he was joined by Sherin. In November of 1993, on a cold day in Brussels, they were married.

The two and a half million pound transformation of the ballroom took two years to complete. The couple were at the heart of the team, planning the kitchen, taking part in every aspect of the operation from the building works to the selection of the cutlery. Nor did their sleepless nights end with the opening of the restaurant in February 1996.

Part of the concept for London was the unique featuring of Créole dishes from the erstwhile French trading posts on the sub-continent. By far the largest remaining community was in Pondicherry. Sherin and Mehernosh went there to investigate. To their delight they discovered that the charming small city on the south eastern coast does indeed retain a French flavour in every sense. A surprising number of dishes had retained a French twist with the potential to provide a unique addition to the restaurant's already wide variety of regional specialities. The contribution of this innovative concept to the outstanding qualities of the Porte des Indes menu was soon acknowledged and the restaurant won both the praise of critics and a string of awards.

Below: La Porte des Indes' team of regional Indian chefs, unrivalled by any other restaurant in London.

13

wine and indian cuisine

LET THE GRAPE VARIETIES GUIDE YOU

It's a widely held belief that beer makes one of the best accompaniments to Indian food. And we wouldn't dispute that a fine lager sometimes hits the spot. Other people, including the majority of the population of the sub-continent, choose fruit juices, *lassi* – that refreshing yoghurt-based concoction – or simply water. However, long ago, when most of Europe was sunk in the dark ages, Indians were drinking wine. Vineyards were concentrated in the west of the country, in Rajasthan to the north and in the valleys of Maharashtra in the centre. With the arrival of the Muslims, late in the 12th century, wine-making came to an end. Recent years have seen a revival of wine-making, but mostly of indifferent quality, though one grower does stand out.

With our company roots in wine-drinking Europe, we've always advocated wine with Indian food at La Porte des Indes. Our list is based on the types of wine we think accompany it best and on a careful choice of growers. As a rule of thumb we think it's best to pick wines that are themselves spicy to match the dishes, or redolent with ripe fruit. To temper the spiciness of the food they are likely to be less dry than the

wines you might choose to complement a European meal. And pronounced tannin should be avoided in the reds. Resist the temptation to serve your wines too cold. A temperature of 12°C to 15°C (53°F to 60°F), that is slightly cool, between cellar and room temperature, is ideal, except for the very fullest reds which may need a degree or two more to bring out all their richness.

In the following suggestions we've mainly given pride of place to the varieties of grape that give individual wines their particular character.

The Traminer grape is mainly grown in Alsace and is used to make wine of the same name as well as Gewürztraminer, a wine so sweet and spicy that some people find it more appropriate as an apéritif. However, surely the ultimate apéritif wine has to be Champagne. Made from a blend of Pinot Noir, Chardonnay and sometimes the less characterful Pinot Meunier, each house blends its Champagne to produce a distinctive style. When you find the one you prefer, stick with it. The best quality Champagnes contain more Chardonnay and no Pinot Meunier in their blends.

For white wine to accompany your food, the Semillon grape gives very aromatic and spicy wines like Bergerac or Semillon Woodcutters White and Watervale Semillon, both from Australia. Half of all Austria's vineyards are planted with the Gruner Vetliner grape which produces light, dry and peppery wines such as the Hinter der Brug Festderspiel on our list. Another interesting and somewhat rare grape grown in the Rhone valley is Viognier, from which wine of subtlety and fragrance is made.

The Sauvignon Blanc white grape produces wine with a fresh grassy taste and a rich body especially when grown in New Zealand. Try a glass of Drylands Sauvignon Blanc with Parsee Fish (page 32) – it's an interesting match. The Cortese grape variety from Piedmont is used to make Gavi, a clean, subtle, refined wine that is a perfect match with seafood recipes such as Crab Malabar (page 35). Pinot Gris, a grape related to Chardonnay, is harvested late by the small Willi Opitz estate in Austria to produce a rich, concentrated wine with a nice acidity – the perfect accompaniment to scallops as prepared in Demoiselles de Pondicherry (page 38).

Chardonnay achieves a concentrated richness over time in California, especially if judiciously oaked. It's a good match for the richness of lobster. You might even switch to red wine to accompany Lobster Anarkali (page 63), in which case you couldn't do better than a Zinfandel, a uniquely Californian grape and super fruity. E&J Gallo are reliable makers of this robust wine that will also go very well with creamy Poulet Rouge (page 82). In Sardinia, winemaker Antonio Argiolas produces a rich, powerful wine from Vermentino grapes. An unusual match might be with Achari Khargosh (page 89), where it will stand up to the strong flavours of the pickling spices used in this recipe for rabbit.

Back to Piedmont with the wine we suggest to accompany Hyderabadi Biryani (page 95): Nebbiolo is one of Italy's finest grape varieties and its intensely fruity, "jammy" character is well expressed in Barolo. Michele Chiarlo makes excellent wine from this grape. But for superbly spicy Pork Vindaloo (page 90), instead of a varietal wine we think that only a blend will suffice. For this we suggest Antonio Argiolas' Turriga made from Cannonau grapes, a Sardinian version of Grenache, and Carignan, a grape more commonly found in France, but also in Spain and California.

For dessert we have a weakness for a rich and jammy Willi Opitz Austrian wine made from Beerenauslese. It goes particularly well with Red Rice *Crème Brûlée* with Jackfruit (page 148) and *Riz au Lait au Confit de Roses* (page 140). For a richer dessert like Star Anise Chocolate Mousse (page 139), instead of wine we suggest Grand Marnier 150 Ans, a superb orange liqueur. And fine old rum, 1919 Angostura, is a superb complement to Chocolate and Chikki Kulfi (page 146).

Finally, back to India at the foot of the Nandi hills, some 40 km from the city of Bangalore, a site chosen after extensive research into soil and weather across the sub-continent. Here, Kanwal K. Grover had 35 varieties of French wine grapes grown for five years to determine which ones would be most suitable. Nine were finally chosen and planted. Top French wine experts were at hand throughout the long gestation of Grover Vineyards wines, first marketed in 1992, nine years after its inception. Today, still backed by French expertise, the vineyards produce excellent red and rosé wines from Cabernet Sauvignon and a Blanc de Blanc from Clairette grapes. It's a drop in the ocean, but at least now it is possible to order Indian wines that match the quality of fine Indian cuisine.

a treasury of teas

A GUIDE TO THE TEAS OF INDIA

It's impossible to travel the highways of India without making regular stops for *chai*. This tea, stewed together with milk, spices and a lot of sugar, is poured from a ladle in an unerringly accurate stream into a beaker an arm's length below, aerating the syrupy brew. *Chai* is not everybody's cup of tea, as it were, but if you want to experience it you can't beat our recipe for *Chai Masala* opposite.

India's variety of climates and landscapes provides the ideal conditions for a wide range of superb teas, from the Himalayas and the slopes of Darjeeling in the north to Nilgiri's blue mountains in the south. The bushes, trimmed to a metre or so (about 3 feet) in height, carpet the slopes in a rich green. In the picking season the young, tender leaves – the best tips – are plucked every few days.

When it comes to the finest teas, selection is of the essence. The majority of the teas served at La Porte des Indes come from a seemingly unlikely source. Just south of the massive 16th century Purana Qila fort in Delhi is the well-known antique market of Sunder Nagar. In the heart of the market there is a minuscule tea shop called Mittals. Over many years Mittals has acquired a unique reputation as a tea blender. Today it supplies tons of tea annually to connoisseurs all over India and the world.

SOME VARIETIES

ASSAM FLOWERY ORANGE PEKOE is a high quality classic leaf tea with a rich, malty character and full flavour.

HIMALAYAN LEAF TEA is a long leaf tea, full bodied and distinctive.

NILGIRI HIGH ELEVATION is a carefully selected flowery pekoe which produces a golden liquor and fine aromatic flavour.

DARJEELING GREEN TEA a greenish, yellow-coloured tea with a bright, refreshing taste.

MUSCATEL DARJEELING TEA is of the highest quality and produces a brew of uniquely distinctive flavour.

MAKING TEA

First rinse out the teapot with boiling water. Put 1 heaped tsp of tea per person into the pot, or to taste, and add boiling water, enough for 2 cups per person. Allow to stand for 3 minutes. Stir briefly and stand for a further 2 minutes. Serve.

Every Indian family has its own recipe for chai masala. They are handed down to daughters when they marry. This is our own Porte des Indes recipe.

chai masala

MAKES 4 CUPS

4 tsp dark Assam tea (you may also use flowery orange
   pekoe or dust as opposed to leaf)
300 ml/½ pint full cream milk
300 ml/½ pint cold water
4 tsp sugar or crushed jaggery, or to taste

La Porte des Indes spice mix
4 pods green cardamom, crushed
1 cm/³⁄₈ in length cinnamon stick
2 cloves

Optional spices*
6 black peppercorns
½ tsp cumin seeds
2½ cm /1 in length lemongrass
2½ cm /1 in length ginger
2–3 small sprigs mint

Put all the ingredients into a saucepan, bring to the boil and simmer for 2–3 minutes. Strain into cups.

* You can enliven your chai masala with your own choice of spices. Use separately as and when required.

Spices are said to have certain beneficial properties:
Peppercorns are said to warm in winter
Lemongrass helps to protect against complaints of the rainy season
Ginger eases coughs and relieves sore throats
Cumin helps to settle the stomach

the indian kitchen

THE STORE CUPBOARD

The extensive palette of spices called for in Indian cookery is perhaps the most daunting impediment to cooks who want to add an Asian dimension to their repertoire. The need for dried spices to be freshly obtained is often emphasised but greatly exaggerated in the opinion of the writers of this book. *Most dried spices kept in air-tight containers will keep almost indefinitely!* Most fresh herbs will keep for at least five days in the refrigerator wrapped in a perforated plastic or preferably a paper bag. Alternatively blanch them by placing them in a sieve and pouring boiling water over them, quickly followed by cold water. Then pat dry and place in a sealed container or bag for deep-freezing. Frozen, they will keep for up to three months.

The most frequently used flavouring ingredients of all are ginger and garlic – too commonplace to be listed below. So many recipes call for a paste made from these two ingredients and a little water to moisten that you may find it worthwhile to make it in a larger quantity and store it in the refrigerator for up to a week, or in the freezer for up to three months.

A subtle use of flavouring ingredients is at the very heart of Indian cookery. The distinctions between fresh and dried, whole and ready powdered, dry roasted and powdered just before use, are important and should be adhered to if you want your dishes to be authentic.

The asterisks in the list below indicate the most frequently used dry flavouring ingredients in the recipes in this book. You may wish to have them permanently to hand. The remainder can be obtained as and when required.

AJWAIN

Ajwain or Ajowan, also known as carom seed, comes in the form of dried seeds, alike in appearance to cumin. The taste is similar to a licoricy thyme. Dried thyme may be substituted.

CARDAMOM*

There are three types of cardamom: green, black and white. It is always sold dried and is available as whole pods or seeds, whole or ground.

CHILLIES*

While there may be more varieties of chilli than there are weeks in the year, the type most often used in Indian cookery and generally referred to in this book is the cayenne chilli. It is slim, around 5 cm/2 in long, red or green, and available fresh or dried. Always be careful when handling chillies. Wear rubber gloves preferably. If not, on no account rub your eyes before having washed and scrubbed your hands.

CINNAMON*

The dried inner bark of the cinnamon tree, it comes in curled sticks to be broken to the lengths required in the recipes.

CORIANDER/CILANTRO*

The fresh leaves look rather similar to flat parsley but the taste is quite different. The dried seeds and powder have completely different flavours from each other and one cannot be substituted for the other.

CUMIN/JEERA*

Small, dried caraway-type seeds, available whole or powdered. This is perhaps the most frequently used spice of all and, indeed, a little powder can also give an interesting lift to European soups and stews.

CURRY LEAVES*

Available both fresh and dry, they have an aroma similar to curry and are widely used, especially in South Indian dishes.

FENUGREEK

Fenugreek is available in several forms: leaves, fresh or dried, and seeds, whole or powdered. Only the leaves and the powdered version are featured in this book. Its taste and smell are powerful and sustained.

GARAM MASALA POWDER*

Garam masala is a blend of spices and is the spice mix most frequently used in Indian cooking. The word *garam* means strongly spicy and *masala* means mix. There are many versions available commercially. This is La Porte Des Indes own recipe, which will keep indefinitely if stored in an airtight container away from heat and sunlight:

MAKES ABOUT 4 TBSP

1 tbsp green cardamom seeds
1 tsp black cardamom seeds
1 tsp cloves
1 tsp black cumin seeds
$\frac{1}{3}$ of a nutmeg
3–4 blades mace
5–7.5 cm/2–3 in stick cinnamon

Grind all the ingredients together as finely as possible in a spice or coffee grinder.

GHEE

Ghee is butter, clarified so that it does not burn when heated to high temperatures. It is readily available at Indian grocers.

VEGETABLE GHEE

A ghee produced from vegetable oil, similar to low cholesterol margarine.

GRAM FLOUR

Also known as chickpea flour.

JAGGERY

Jaggery is the juice of sugarcane, reduced until it forms a crumbly mass. Unrefined, it has a unique flavour and is available at Indian grocers. Demerara sugar can be substituted if necessary.

LENTILS AND CHICKPEAS/DAL*

Lentils and chickpeas, both classified as *dal* (sometimes spelt *dhal*), are a staple food in India and available in many varieties. Those used in this book are: *toor dal* – yellow lentils, *channa dal* – yellow chickpeas, *masoor dal* – red lentils, *urad dal* – black lentils, *kala chana* – black chickpeas.

MUSTARD SEEDS*

A frequently used ingredient, they are often the prelude to preparing a dish, thrown into hot oil in the pan and left for a few seconds until they "pop", immediately after which other ingredients are added.

PANEER

Paneer is similar to cottage cheese, which is an acceptable substitute. To make your own paneer, heat full cream milk until it boils. Remove pan from the heat and add lemon juice. This will curdle the milk. Separate the solid curds from the liquid (whey) by straining through muslin placed in a sieve over a basin. Then put the curds between two plates and place a weight over. Set aside for several hours until the remaining whey has been extracted and the paneer sets. It is then ready for use. Paneer can be stored in the refrigerator for several days. 2 tbsp of lemon juice should be enough to curdle 450 ml/15 fl oz/2 cups of milk and produce 150 g/5 oz of paneer.

PAPRIKA*

A mild powder made from red peppers/pimentos.

SAFFRON*

This legendary spice is the dried stigma of the crocus, hand-picked at dawn and literally worth its weight in gold. Happily you will never need to use more than a tiny amount. While there may be other ways of colouring your dish saffron yellow, there is no substitute for its unique taste.

STAR ANISE

This pretty star-shaped spice is the dried flower of a tree found only in China. It is occasionally used, ground, in Indian cookery.

TAMARIND*

Tamarind is the pulp found inside the pods of the tamarind tree that surrounds the seeds. It is available both in the form of a fibrous block and as a paste. To use a piece of the block, soak in warm water to soften and pass through a sieve.

TURMERIC*

One of the most frequently used spices, turmeric is a member of the ginger family. The roots are dried and almost invariably ground into a powder for use in cooking. It gives the characteristically yellow hue to many dishes.

VADAVAM (VADOUVAN)

A mixture of spices used in Southern India and in the Créole cookery of Pondicherry. This is La Porte Des Indes own recipe, which is also an important ingredient of the duck recipe on page 81.

MAKES 120 G/4 OZ

100 g/3½ oz Spanish onion, crushed with the
    juice retained
60 g/2 oz garlic, peeled and crushed with
    the juice retained
10–15 sprigs fresh curry leaves, crushed with the
    juice retained
4 tbsp masoor dal (red lentils)
4 tbsp split urad dal (black lentils)
4 tsp fenugreek
4 tsp mustard seeds

Mix all the ingredients together, spread them out on a baking tray and, if the weather is sunny and dry, leave exposed outside to the sun all day. At sundown, bring indoors, roll the ingredients into balls, cover and leave overnight. Repeat the procedure until all moisture has evaporated, 3 to 4 days.

Alternatively, place the baking tray in a very slow oven – the setting you use to heat plates – and leave for several hours, repeating, like the sun-drying procedure, until all the moisture has evaporated, again after 3 to 4 days.

EQUIPMENT

If you cook regularly, you probably already have all the equipment you really need to produce Indian dishes in your kitchen. This will include at least one frying pan and good quality, thick bottomed saucepans with lids, a deep fryer (we strongly recommend an electric deep fryer for accurate temperature control and safety), a grater, a pestle and mortar and, if possible, a food processor. Plus, of course, sharp knives, a slotted spoon, chopping boards, etc.

A very desirable piece of equipment is a deep wok-shaped pan with handles called a *karahi*. A conventional wok with a lid will do very well and an electric wok with a thermostat even better. (A conventional wok used on an electric hotplate, however, is not satisfactory. It does not achieve the necessary high temperature for the quick dry-roasting that is often involved in preparing Indian dishes.)

Last, but not least, you may feel the need for an efficient extractor hood over the stove or, failing that, a nearby open window!

A NOTE ABOUT COOKING TIMES

Please note that the cooking times provided in our recipes should, for the most part, be used as a guide. In practice several variables can affect cooking times, from variations in individual equipment to altitude. We recommend testing "doneness" with a fork and taste testing, as you would do with any other type of cuisine. Spicy stewed dishes will become milder in flavour the longer they are cooked.

HORS D'OEUVRES

There's a knack to making this typical Bombay street food
and our Maharashtrian Chef Subash Rewale, who contributed
this recipe, certainly has it. See if you can acquire it too!

bombay savoury street snack
SEV BATATA PURI

**MAKES ABOUT 24 POORIES (SAVOURY
BISCUITS) AND THEIR TOPPINGS**

For the green chutney
60 g/2oz fresh coriander leaves
2 fresh green chillies
1 clove garlic
½ tsp cumin powder
2 tbsp lemon juice
Salt to taste

For the tamarind chutney
60 g/2 oz tamarind block
1.5 cm/½ in length finger of ginger, peeled
1.5 cm/½ in length cinnamon stick
80 g/3 oz jaggery

For the poories
20 g/⅔ oz vegetable ghee, melted
100 g/3½ oz plain flour
½ tsp salt
Vegetable oil, to deep-fry

For the garnish
1 medium potato, boiled and mashed
4 tbsp thick yoghurt, with 1 tbsp sugar whisked in
60 g/2 oz sev*
½ medium red onion, finely chopped
1 medium green mango, finely chopped
1 tbsp fresh coriander leaves, chopped
Juice of 1 lemon

Blend or process the green chutney ingredients together into a fine paste.

Boil the tamarind, ginger and cinnamon in water until soft, about 20 to 30 minutes. Drain and pass through a sieve. Add the jaggery and simmer gently for 5 to 10 minutes.

To make the poorie bases, mix the melted ghee into the salted flour, adding enough water to form a fairly soft dough. Roll it thinly and cut into about 24 × 4 cm/1¾ in discs with a circular cutter. Heat the oil to 180°C/350°F. Prick the discs with a fork and deep-fry in batches until they are golden brown, about 2 to 3 minutes. Drain well.

To assemble the poories and their toppings, first spread the poories with the mashed potato. Top with ½ tsp each of chutney and the sweetened yoghurt. Sprinkle with the sev, chopped onion, mango and coriander leaves and squeeze over a few drops of lemon juice.

* Sev are thin, deep-fried gram flour noodles, obtainable from Indian grocers.

Chard, also known as Swiss chard, is a thick-stemmed leaf vegetable related to beetroot. The leaves can be either red or green, and both are put to colourful use in this original recipe created by Mehernosh Mody. The stalks of the chard, not used in this recipe, can be boiled or steamed and served in the same ways as asparagus.

chard and water chestnut pakora

MAKES 8-9 PIECES

150 g/5 oz red chard leaves
150 g/5 oz green chard leaves
150 g/5 oz water chestnuts, very finely chopped (drained tinned water chestnuts are suitable if you can't find fresh)
4 tbsp gram flour
1 tsp roasted cumin powder
½ tsp red chilli powder
½ tsp ajwain
½ tsp turmeric
Salt to taste
Vegetable oil, for deep-frying
1 tsp chaat masala
Mango sauce (see page 131), to serve

Cut the chard leaves into 2.5 cm/1 in wide strips, wash well in cold water, drain and pat dry.

Combine all the remaining ingredients except the oil and chaat masala and mix well with the chard leaves. Using the palms of your hands, form 9–10 balls about 2.5 cm/1 in diameter, then flatten the balls. Heat the oil to 180°C/350°F and deep-fry pakoras until crisp, about 1½–2 minutes.

Pat the pakoras with paper kitchen roll to remove excess oil, sprinkle with the chaat masala and serve hot, with mango sauce.

Crisp batter contrasts with melting cheese and moist, fresh-tasting aubergine in this Créole version of an Indian *pakora*.

aubergine fritters
BEIGNETS D'AUBERGINE

MAKES 12

2 medium aubergines weighing about 125 g/4 oz each
80 g/3 oz Gruyère or Cheddar cheese, grated
4 tbsp paneer or cottage cheese
½ green pepper, seeded and grated
½ red pepper, seeded and grated
½ tsp cumin powder
½ tsp paprika powder
Salt
120 g/4 oz gram flour
1 pinch bicarbonate of soda
½ tsp ajwain seeds
Vegetable oil, to deep-fry
Tamarind sauce (see page 132), to serve

Slice the aubergines 1 cm/¼ in thick, then slit each slice horizontally, leaving an edge uncut to hold the two halves together.

Mix together the grated cheese and paneer or cottage cheese. Squeeze any moisture out of the grated peppers and add them to the cheeses with the powdered spices. Add salt to taste, mix well and spread the cheese mixture into the pockets you have made in the aubergine slices.

Mix the gram flour with a pinch of bicarbonate of soda, the ajwain seeds and a pinch of salt and slowly mix in enough water to make a thick, smooth batter.

Heat the deep-frying oil to 170°C/325°F. Dip the stuffed aubergine pockets into the batter and deep-fry until golden brown, about 3 to 4 minutes. Serve hot with tamarind sauce.

The universal snack, enjoyed all over India – north, south, east and west! This recipe combines the tastiest of regional ingredients.

vegetable samosas
SHINGORA

MAKES 12

For the filling
150 g/5 oz large red-skinned potatoes, peeled and chopped into the smallest possible dice
½ tsp turmeric powder
2 tbsp vegetable oil
1 bay leaf
1.5 cm/½ in length cinnamon stick
½ tsp cumin seeds
100 g/3½ oz carrots, grated
100 g/3½ oz cauliflower florets, finely chopped
½ tsp garam masala powder (see page 19)
½ tsp red chilli powder
100 g/3½ oz green peas

For the dough
100 g/3½ oz plain flour
Pinch of salt
2½ tbsp vegetable ghee
Vegetable oil, to deep-fry
Tamarind sauce (see page 132), to serve

Boil the diced potatoes with the salt and turmeric until just done, about 5 minutes, and drain.

Heat the 2 tbsp vegetable oil in a pan and fry the bay leaf, cinnamon and cumin seeds for about 10 seconds, then mix the grated vegetables in well and add the garam masala and red chilli powders. Stir-fry over medium heat until the vegetables are cooked, about 5 minutes. Mix in the peas and boiled potatoes, cook for a further 2 minutes, adding salt to taste. Remove the bay leaf and set aside to cool.

To make the dough, sift the flour into a bowl, adding a little salt. Work in the vegetable ghee with your fingers and add a little water, kneading the mixture to a medium-firm dough. Divide the dough into 3 balls and roll each out to a thin circle. Cut each circle into 4 segments and form each segment into a cone, moistening an edge to seal.

Fill the cones with the vegetable mixture and moisten the top of the cone to seal, forming a pouch and crimping the sides. Heat the oil to 170°C/325°F and deep-fry the samosas in batches until golden brown, 4 to 5 minutes. Serve with tamarind sauce.

This dish of little dumplings from North India can be served alone or as a soothing accompaniment to a spicy curry.

lentil dumplings in a yoghurt sauce
DAHI WADA

MAKES 16

100 g/3½ oz urad dal (skinned and split black lentils)
½ fresh green chilli, finely chopped
1.5 cm/½ in length finger of ginger, peeled and
    finely chopped
Salt to taste
200 ml/7 fl oz yoghurt
½ tsp cumin seeds
1 pinch sugar
Vegetable oil, to deep-fry
4–5 tbsp tamarind sauce (see page 132)
Fresh chopped coriander leaves, to garnish

Soak the dal in warm water for 1 hour. Drain and process to a smooth paste using a minimum of water. Add the finely chopped green chilli, ginger and salt and mix well.

Heat the oil to 180°C/350°F. Using a teaspoon, make small round balls of the dal mixture and drop them into the oil. Fry until they are golden brown, about 4 to 5 minutes. Remove and drain on absorbent kitchen paper as they are done.

Dry-roast the cumin seeds briefly, taking care not to burn them, then crush them to a powder. Whisk the powder, sugar and a little salt into the yoghurt. Taste and adjust seasoning.

Place the deep-fried dumplings in slightly salted warm water for 10 minutes, then press them gently between the palms of your hands to flatten them slightly and remove the moisture.

To serve, divide the dumplings between 4 individual bowls, pour yoghurt all over them, top with tamarind sauce and garnish with the coriander leaves.

Chef Mehernosh Mody learned this classic Parsee wedding dish from his mother. Lemon sole replaces traditional pomfret and marries beautifully with the mint and coconut-rich mixture enclosed in banana leaf parcels.

parsee steamed fish
PATRA NI MACHI

SERVES 4

1 good-sized lemon sole, cut into 4 fillets
1 tsp salt
1 tsp pepper
Juice of ½ lemon
½ bunch fresh coriander
2–3 sprigs mint
1 green chilli, roughly chopped
½ tsp cumin seeds
2 garlic cloves, peeled and chopped
2 tbsp freshly grated coconut*
1 banana leaf

Season the fillets with salt and pepper rubbed in with a little of the lemon juice and set aside.

Make a chutney by pounding or processing to a fine paste the coriander, mint, green chilli, cumin seeds and garlic. Add the grated coconut, the rest of the lemon juice and salt to taste.

Cut the banana leaf into four sheets large enough to fold into parcels around the fish. Spread the coconut mixture over the fillets, fold them to form 4 sandwiches, place them on the banana leaf sheets and fold the banana sheets over the fillets to form parcels. (An alternative method would be to wrap the fish in kitchen parchment paper.)

Steam the parcels until the fish is cooked, about 5 to 7 minutes and serve hot.

* To make the chutney for authentic Parsee fish there is no substitute for fresh coconut. Chop the coconut in two with a cleaver and remove the flesh by sliding a sharp knife between it and the hard shell. Then grate it with a regular grater. This may seem a great deal of trouble to take to prepare one dish, but you can make a larger quantity of chutney and keep the remainder in the freezer for up to 1 month.

Nooror Somany, key founder of La Porte des Indes, created
this dish of crabmeat infused with coconut and southern spices.
The dish can be served, warm or cold, in the crab shells if you
bought whole crabs, and garnished with the fried curry leaves.

crab malabar

SERVES 4

2 tbsp vegetable oil
½ tsp mustard seeds
½ tsp poppy seeds
1 stem curry leaves
½ Spanish onion, chopped
4 garlic cloves, peeled and finely chopped
½ tsp turmeric powder
3 tbsp yoghurt
120 ml/4 fl oz coconut milk
2 tbsp desiccated coconut
200 g/7 oz fresh or frozen crab meat, flaked and with
    moisture gently pressed out
2 tbsp sweet corn kernels
Salt to taste
Fried curry leaves, to garnish

Heat the oil in a pan. Put in the mustard seeds and when they splutter after a few seconds add the poppy seeds. After a further few seconds add the curry leaves followed by the chopped onion and fry gently until the onion is translucent. Add the chopped garlic and sauté a further minute.

Add the turmeric powder and sauté for 10 seconds before lowering the heat and adding the yoghurt. Simmer for a bare minute then add the coconut milk and the desiccated coconut. Continue to simmer for 3 to 4 minutes to reduce. Stir in crab meat and corn kernels, return to the boil and check seasoning, adding salt to taste. Serve garnished with fried curry leaves.

This recipe is a creation of Chef Mehernosh Mody.

pepper crabs

SERVES 4

12 soft shell crabs*
2 tsp finely ground black pepper
½ tsp turmeric powder
½ tsp chilli powder
60 g/2 oz rice flour
Vegetable oil, to deep-fry
Chopped fresh coriander leaves, to garnish

For the sauce
2 tbsp vegetable oil
1 red onion, chopped
4 garlic cloves, peeled and finely chopped
1 tsp fresh green peppercorns
1 tsp dry pink peppercorns
Juice of ½ lemon
Salt to taste

Sprinkle the crabs with black pepper, turmeric and chilli powders and coat with rice flour. Heat the oil to 180°C/350°F and deep-fry the crabs for 2 to 3 minutes until they are crisp and light brown. Drain on absorbent kitchen paper.

For the sauce, heat 2 tbsp vegetable oil in a pan, add the onion and chopped garlic and sauté over high heat until crisp, about 2 minutes. Add the green and pink peppercorns and toss together. Add the crabs, toss again in the mixture, adding lemon juice and salt. Serve immediately, garnished with the coriander leaves.

* Soft shell crabs are obtainable deep-frozen at Asian supermarkets.

Cynthia De Souza, a good friend and an excellent cook,

inspired this typically south western recipe of crunchy,

golden fried giant prawns.

spicy semolina crumbed prawns
JHINGA JALPARI

SERVES 4

4 garlic cloves, peeled and chopped
1 tbsp cumin seeds
10–12 dried red chillies
45 g/1½ oz mustard seeds
2 tbsp malt vinegar
16 raw king prawns, heads removed
1 egg
1½ tbsp cornflour
90 g/3 oz semolina
Salt, to taste
Vegetable oil, to deep-fry
Karwari coconut chutney (see page 134), to serve

Soak the garlic, cumin seeds, red chillies and mustard seeds in the vinegar for 2 to 3 hours before blending or processing to a fine, smooth paste.

Shell the prawns, leaving the last segment of the shell with the tail in place. De-vein the prawns by making an incision along the back and lifting out the black, thread-like vein. Then form each prawn into a circle, securing the shape by pushing the tail through the flesh and into the channel made by removing the vein. Coat each prawn with the paste and set aside for at least two hours.

Beat the egg in a bowl. Mix the cornflour, semolina and salt together in another bowl. Dip each prawn first into the egg and then into the cornflour and semolina, making sure it is well coated.

Heat the oil to 180°C/350°F and deep-fry prawns in batches until golden brown, 2 to 3 minutes. Serve with Karwari coconut chutney.

A creamy curry and saffron sauce perfectly complements the firm flesh and clean taste of fresh scallops.

scallops in a saffron sauce
DEMOISELLES DE PONDICHERRY

SERVES 4

8 king-sized scallops
1 pinch salt
1½ tsp curry powder
30 g/1 oz butter
2 garlic cloves, peeled and finely chopped
½ medium-sized Spanish onion, chopped
5–6 curry leaves
1 pinch ground white pepper
1 pinch saffron strands
250 ml/9 fl oz double cream
1 tbsp vegetable oil
Fried curry leaves, to garnish

Season the scallops with salt and ½ tsp curry powder and set aside.

Heat the butter in a pan. Put in the chopped garlic and sweat over a low heat until it is golden brown. Add the chopped onion and fry until it is translucent. Add the curry leaves, remaining curry powder, pepper and saffron. Stir for 1 minute, then add the cream and continue to stir gently until the mixture begins to thicken. Add salt to taste.

In another thick-bottomed pan, heat the oil and sear the scallops for about 30 seconds on each side, or longer according to taste. Place them on the sauce and serve hot, garnished with the fried curry leaves.

As simple and elegant as a spring roll,

fresh grated vegetables lighten this

original version of a classic Indian samosa.

chicken samosas
SUNHERE SAMOSA

MAKES 12

3–4 garlic cloves, peeled and finely chopped
2.5 cm/1 in length finger of ginger, peeled and
   finely chopped
2 tbsp vegetable oil
1.5 cm/½ in length cinnamon stick
1 bay leaf
½ tsp chilli powder
½ tsp turmeric powder
30 g/1 oz carrot, grated
30 g/1 oz cauliflower florets, finely chopped
350 g/11½ oz minced chicken
30 g/1 oz sweetcorn kernels
½ tsp garam masala powder (see page 19)
Salt to taste
3 sheets spring roll pastry, each 25 × 25 cm/10 × 10 in
1 egg, beaten
Vegetable oil, to deep-fry
Mango sauce (see page 131), to serve

Pound the chopped garlic and ginger into a paste with a little water. Heat 2 tbsp vegetable oil and add the cinnamon and bay leaf followed by the garlic and ginger paste. Fry until the paste is lightly browned, 3–4 minutes, then lower the heat and add the chilli and turmeric powders, mixing well.

Add the grated carrot and cauliflower. Stir-fry for a minute and then add the minced chicken, stirring thoroughly to ensure the mince is not lumpy. Continue to stir over a low heat until all the moisture has evaporated, about 15 minutes, then add the sweetcorn, garam masala powder and salt to taste and cook for a further 2 minutes. Set aside to cool.

Cut the spring roll pastry sheets into strips 6 cm/2¼ in wide. Fold one end of each strip twice diagonally to make a triangular pouch and put in a little of the filling. Fold the remaining length of the strip over and over to close the pouch and seal with beaten egg.

Heat the deep-frying oil to 170°C/325°F and deep-fry the samosas until golden brown, about 2 minutes. Serve with mango sauce.

This recipe for crisp, deep-fried mushroom rissoles was created by Mehernosh Mody. You can try it with your own combination of mushroom varieties.

mushroom rissoles
KHUMB KA KABAB

MAKES 10

100 g/3½ oz potatoes, peeled
2 garlic cloves, peeled and chopped
1 tbsp vegetable oil
½ tsp turmeric powder
1 scant tsp chilli powder
400 g/14 oz button mushrooms, roughly chopped
100 g/3½ oz oyster mushrooms, roughly chopped
1 tsp lemon juice
2 tsp chaat masala powder
Salt to taste
2 tbsp cornflour
White breadcrumbs, to coat
Vegetable oil, to deep-fry
Tomato chutney (see page 135), to serve

Boil the potatoes until soft, about 25 minutes. Mash without adding any other ingredient.

Pound the garlic with a little water to form a paste. Heat 1 tbsp vegetable oil in a pan, add the garlic paste and sauté until light brown, then add the turmeric and chilli powders and sauté *for two seconds only* before adding all the chopped mushrooms. Stir continuously over medium heat until all moisture has evaporated. Add the lemon juice and set aside to cool.

Add the mashed potato and chaat masala to the cooled mushroom mixture, season with salt, mix well together and form into 10 flat round cakes about 5 cm/2 in diameter.

Mix the cornflour with enough water to make a thin batter. Dip the cakes into the batter and then roll them in the breadcrumbs, ensuring that they are evenly coated. Heat the oil to 160°C/320°F and fry the rissoles until golden brown, 1 to 2 minutes. Serve with tomato chutney.

A delightful garlicky starter with an appealing green colour.

chicken kebabs
CHICKEN LASOONI TIKKA

SERVES 4

4 chicken breast fillets, skinned
10 garlic cloves, peeled
1.25 cm/½ in length fresh ginger
Salt
Juice of ½ lemon
1½ tbsp vegetable oil
250ml/9 fl oz thick yoghurt
½ tsp garam masala powder (see page 19)
2 blades mace
3 pods green cardamom
2 green chillies, seeded for a milder taste
    and finely chopped
1 tsp cornflour
1 tbsp spinach purée
Mint sauce (see page 132), to serve
Lemon wedges, to garnish

Cut the chicken breasts into 2.5 cm/1 in cubes.

Take two of the garlic cloves and chop finely with the ginger, add a little water and process or pound in a mortar into a smooth paste. (You may find it practical to make this paste in larger quantities and store the surplus in a jar with a tight-fitting lid in the refrigerator for subsequent use.)

Rub salt, lemon juice and the ginger and garlic paste into the cubed chicken breasts and set aside.

Finely chop the remaining garlic cloves, heat the oil in a pan, and fry them light brown. Set aside to cool.

In a mixing bowl, whisk the fried garlic into the yoghurt with the garam masala, mace, cardamom pods, chopped chilli, cornflour and spinach purée. Stir in the chicken cubes and leave to marinate for 2 hours.

Thread the chicken cubes on to four skewers and place under a heated grill in mid-position. Grill for 5 to 6 minutes, turning so that each side is exposed to the heat. Serve with mint sauce and garnish with lemon wedges.

Chef Ibrahim Abdoulakime from Pondicherry specializes in *hors d'oeuvres* and added the exotic touches to this French mixed salad. If you can't find fresh banana flowers, they are available tinned in Chinese supermarkets.

banana flower salad
SALADE DU MÉTIS

SERVES 4

2 chicken breast fillets, skinned
Salt and white pepper
Vegetable oil, to deep-fry
4 garlic cloves, peeled and chopped
2 tbsp vegetable oil, to sauté
100 g/3½ oz button mushrooms, sliced
2 handfuls mixed salad leaves (wild rocket, oak leaf,
   lamb's lettuce, treviso etc., according to availability)
1 tsp tamarind pulp
1 banana flower
Juice of ½ lemon
8 cherry tomatoes halved, to garnish.

Rub the chicken breasts with salt and white pepper and steam until tender, about 15 minutes. Allow to cool and cut into long, thin shreds.

Heat the oil for deep-frying to 160°C/320°F and cook the garlic until it is light brown. Drain on kitchen paper and set aside.

Heat 2 tbsp vegetable oil in a frying pan and sauté the mushrooms until cooked, 4 to 5 minutes. Drain the mushrooms, reserving the cooking liquid.

Wash and dry the salad leaves, tearing the larger ones into smaller pieces. Divide them between four plates to make a base. Make a dressing with the retained cooking liquid, the garlic, tamarind pulp, lemon juice and salt to taste.

To dress the banana flower, halve it lengthways, cut off the base and remove the brown outer leaves and the inner core, retaining the tender leaves. Shred the latter and put them straight away into a bowl of water acidulated with a little lemon juice to prevent them turning brown.

Mix together the shredded chicken, mushrooms and banana flower and toss in the dressing. Arrange the dressed mixture on the salad leaves and garnish with the cherry tomatoes.

tandoori foie gras

Here's a highly creative way of preparing raw foie gras, but, given the rarity and cost of the principal ingredient, not to be undertaken lightly. To employ the traditional *dunghaar* smoking method you will need a piece of glowing charcoal, for which you will in turn need a barbecue, for example a *Hibachi* for use indoors.

SERVES 4

For the chutney
2 tbsp vegetable oil
2 dry red chillies
2.5 cm/1 in length cinnamon stick
1 spring onion, sliced
1.5 cm/½ in length finger of ginger
30 g/1 oz jaggery or cane sugar
150 g/5 oz tamarind pulp
4 dates, preferably medjool, stoned and puréed

Half a lobe of raw foie gras, weighing about 350 g/
    12 oz, cut into 8 slices about 1.25cm/½ in thick
30g/1 oz butter, for frying
1 star anise
1 tsp butter, melted

The smoking procedure described on the right is called dhungaar *and can be used to smoke other items, for example, salmon steaks, fillets of chicken or splayed quail.*

If you have no means of heating charcoal until it glows it is possible to achieve a similar effect by the following alternative method:

Line your ironware casserole dish with foil and sprinkle a mixture of brown sugar, star anise and cinnamon on top. Place a rack over, close the lid and place the casserole over high heat until the mixture smokes. Then place the slices of foie gras on the rack, close the lid again, remove the casserole from the heat and allow the smoke to flavour the foie gras for 1 minute. Remove the slices of foie gras and serve.

To prepare the chutney, which may be done in advance, heat the oil and put in the whole spices. When they release their aroma after about 10 to 15 seconds, add the spring onions and the ginger. Sauté for 1 minute and then add the jaggery or sugar and stir to dissolve.

Add the tamarind pulp and a little water. Bring to the boil and simmer for 8 to 10 minutes.

Thoroughly push the mixture through a sieve, discarding the residue. Re-heat and add the date purée. Bring to the boil and simmer very gently until the chutney has a thick, jammy consistency, 3 to 5 minutes.

At La Porte des Indes the slices of foie gras are first skewered and then placed in a hot tandoor oven to sear for 30 to 45 seconds. To prepare them in a home kitchen, first heat the butter in a non-stick frying pan until it ceases to bubble and sear the slices of foie gras for about 5 seconds on each side. Then arrange them in an ironware casserole dish with a tight fitting lid. It should be as warm as a heated plate but not hot enough to continue to cook the foie gras. Leave a space in the centre.

Place a glowing piece of charcoal on a small heatproof dish such as a ramekin and place the dish in the space at the centre of the casserole dish. Place a star anise on top of the charcoal and pour the teaspoonful of melted butter over it. Immediately close the lid of the casserole. Leave for 1 to 2 minutes while the slices of foie gras are lightly smoked. Open the lid, taking care not to breathe in the smoke, remove the slices and place them on warm (but not overheated) plates.

Add a dollop of the chutney and serve with naan bread (see page 127).

Puff pastry adds a luxuriously
buttery French element to this minced
lamb pasty.

lamb samosas
RASOUL

MAKES 12

For the filling
2–3 garlic cloves, peeled and finely chopped
4 cm/1½ in length finger of ginger, finely chopped
2 tbsp vegetable oil
1 bay leaf
1.5 cm/½ in length cinnamon stick
½ Spanish onion, peeled and chopped
½ tsp paprika powder
½ tsp coriander powder
1 pinch turmeric powder
375 g/12½ oz lamb, minced
Salt to taste
½ tsp garam masala powder (see page 19)
30 g/1 oz green peas

2 sheets puff pastry (approx. 29 x 37 cm/12 x 14 in)
1 egg, beaten
Sauce Créole à la tomate (see page 134), to serve

For the filling, pound the garlic and ginger with a little water into a paste. Heat the 2 tbsp vegetable oil and put in the bay leaf and the cinnamon. Add the chopped onion and fry until light brown, about 5 minutes. Add the garlic and ginger paste and cook for a further 2 minutes. Lower the heat and add the paprika, coriander and turmeric powders. Mix well.

Add the minced lamb and salt to taste. Stir until the moisture has almost evaporated and the mince is cooked, about 7 minutes. Add the garam masala and then the green peas and stir-fry for a further 2 minutes. Set aside and allow to cool

Heat the oven to 200°C/400°F/Gas Mark 6. Cut out 24 x 7 cm/3 in squares of puff pastry. Place a little pile of the filling in the centre of 12 squares, moisten the edges of the square with beaten egg, place another square over and seal the edges. Brush with the beaten egg.

Arrange the pasties on a baking tray and bake until golden brown, 15–20 minutes. Serve with the sauce Créole à la tomate (see page 134).

A little melted cheese adds an
unexpected note to this classic kebab.

lamb and herb kebabs
LUCKNOWI SEEKH KABAB

SERVES 4

2.5 cm/1 in length finger of ginger, peeled
   and finely chopped
4–5 garlic cloves, peeled and finely chopped
550 g/1 lb 4 oz leg of lamb, diced
1 small red onion, finely chopped
3 green chillies, finely chopped
1½ tsp red chilli powder
½ tsp turmeric
1 tsp coriander powder
2–3 stems fresh coriander, finely chopped
1 tbsp grated cheddar cheese
1 egg
Salt to taste
Vegetable oil, to baste
Chaat masala, to garnish
Mint sauce (see page 132), to serve

Process or pound together the chopped ginger and garlic, adding a little water to make a smooth paste. Mix the paste with the lamb and mince all together, then mix in the onion, green chillies, red chilli, turmeric and coriander powders, coriander, cheese, egg and salt.

Form the mixture into 12 balls and spike them on to four metal skewers. Dip your hands in water and work the balls into sausage shapes, 10–12 cm/4–5 in long.

Place the skewers under the grill in mid-position and cook, turning and basting with oil until they are done, about 4 to 5 minutes. Remove from the heat, sprinkle the kebabs with a little chaat masala and serve with mint sauce.

SOUPS

A refreshing and easily prepared soup served chilled – perfect for Summer. Alfonso mangoes are the best variety to use, but canned ones could be substituted if they prove hard to find.

chilled mango soup

SERVES 4

200 g/7 oz Alfonso mango pulp
  (canned mango pulp may be used)
400 ml/14 fl oz yoghurt
2 tbsp vegetable oil
½ tsp mustard seeds
1.5 cm/½ in length finger of ginger, peeled
  and finely chopped
2 green chillies, finely chopped
10 fresh curry leaves
Salt to taste
Fried curry leaves, to garnish

Whisk the mango pulp together with the yoghurt, adding water if necessary to obtain a not too thick, soupy consistency.

Heat the oil. Put in the mustard seeds and when they pop, after a few seconds, add the ginger, chillies and curry leaves. Stir-fry for 1 minute. Remove from the heat and add to the mango pulp and yoghurt. Check seasoning and add salt to taste. Serve chilled, garnished with fried curry leaves.

pumpkin and roasted garlic soup

SERVES 4

2 tsp butter
500 g/1 lb 2oz pumpkin, peeled and sliced into small pieces
4–5 sprigs fresh coriander leaves and stalks
½ tsp turmeric
1 pinch chilli powder
9–10 garlic cloves, peeled and oven-roasted until soft
    and browned
Salt and white pepper, to season
Cream and chopped chives, to garnish

Melt the butter in a thick-bottomed pan and cook the pumpkin pieces on a low heat for 3 minutes. Add the coriander, turmeric and chilli powder and continue to cook for 1 minute. Add the roasted garlic cloves and 700 ml/ 1¼ pints water, bring to the boil and simmer for 10 to 15 minutes. Purée the soup and season. Serve hot with a swirl of cream and a sprinkling of chopped chives.

yellow lentil soup
DAKSHIN

SERVES 4

100 g/3½ oz masoor dal (red lentils)
100g/3½ oz toor dal (yellow lentils)
2.5 litres/4½ pints water
1 tsp Madras curry powder
½ tsp turmeric powder
2 tbsp vegetable oil
½ tsp mustard seeds
½ medium Spanish onion, chopped
3 garlic cloves, finely chopped
2.5cm/1 in length finger of fresh ginger, finely chopped
1 fresh green chilli, finely chopped
1 fresh red chilli, finely chopped
1 sprig fresh curry leaves
Juice of 1 lime
Salt to taste
Fresh coriander and 4 lemon slices, to garnish

Wash the lentils, cover with the measured water, bring to the boil, add the Madras curry powder and the turmeric powder and boil over medium heat until the lentils are cooked, about 50–55 minutes. Remove from the heat and purée.

Heat the oil and put in the mustard seeds. When they splutter after a few seconds, add the onion and sauté until light brown, then add the garlic and ginger and sauté for a further minute before adding both chillies and the curry leaves. Continue to cook for a further 30 seconds. Add the lentil puree, re-heat and add the lime juice and salt to taste. Serve in soup bowls garnished with the fresh coriander and lemon slices.

Chef Rajesh Dalaya, of La Porte des Indes restaurant in Brussels, perfected the recipe for this full-bodied and meaty winter soup.

lamb shank soup
NALLI KA SHORBA

SERVES 4

4 lamb shanks
5 tbsp vegetable oil
1 tsp peeled and chopped garlic
200 g/7 oz Spanish onion, chopped
2.5 cm/1 in finger of ginger, peeled and finely chopped
1 green chilli, finely chopped
½ tsp red chilli powder
½ tsp coriander powder
200 g/7 oz tomatoes, chopped
Pinch of saffron strands
1 tsp lemon juice
Salt to taste
Chopped fresh coriander leaves, to garnish

For the lamb stock
Lamb bones and trimmings
½ tsp peppercorns
4 cloves
1 bay leaf
1 Spanish onion, roughly chopped
Stalks from ½ bunch fresh coriander

For the marinade
4 garlic cloves, peeled and finely chopped
2.5 cm/1 in length finger of ginger, peeled and finely chopped
½ tsp red chilli powder
½ tsp turmeric powder
Salt

To make the stock, cover the lamb bones and trimmings with cold water, add all the other stock ingredients, bring to the boil and simmer very gently, uncovered, for at least 2 hours, skimming the surface from time to time to remove scum. Pass the simmered stock through a sieve and discard solids.

To make the marinade, pound the chopped garlic and ginger in a mortar together with a little water to make a smooth paste. Mix in the chilli and turmeric powders and some salt. Smear the marinade over the lamb shanks and rub in with your fingers. Set aside for at least 2 hours. (Be careful not to rub your eyes while your fingers are coated in marinade; wash your hands thoroughly afterwards.)

To cook the lamb, heat half the oil in a large saucepan and brown the shanks evenly all over. Add the strained stock, cover and cook over medium heat until the meat is tender, about 25 minutes.

Heat the rest of the oil in another pan and fry the chopped garlic until golden brown. Add the chopped onions and, when they are also golden brown, add the ginger, chopped green chilli, red chilli and coriander powders and, finally the tomatoes. Simmer until the tomatoes are softened, 3 to 4 minutes, then pour it into the pan containing the shanks. Bring back to the boil, add the saffron and simmer for a further 3 to 4 minutes. Add the lemon juice and salt to taste and serve garnished with the chopped fresh coriander leaves.

A smooth and deliciously smoky soup spiked with an infusion of herbs and spices.

smoked tomato and pepper soup

SERVES 4

8–9 garlic cloves
3 medium red peppers
Vegetable oil, to brush
2.5 cm/1 in cinnamon stick
2 green cardamom pods
2 cloves
1 bay leaf
2.5 cm/1 in length finger of ginger, peeled and finely sliced
750 g/1 lb 9 oz tomatoes, halved and base of the stems removed
A few stems fresh coriander
5–6 mint leaves
2 tbsp vegetable oil
1 tsp cumin seeds
1 tsp sugar
Salt to taste
Fresh coriander, to garnish

Preheat the oven to 200°C/400°F. Peel 5 or 6 of the garlic cloves, brush the peppers with vegetable oil and roast these together until cooked, about 25–30 minutes. Skin, seed and roughly chop the peppers.

Wrap the cinnamon, cardamom, cloves, bay leaf and ginger in muslin and tie with string to make a *bouquet garni*.

Bring the tomatoes to the boil in a little water with the roasted garlic, the peppers, the *bouquet garni*, the fresh coriander and the mint leaves. Simmer and reduce to a soupy consistency, about 20–25 minutes. Remove the *bouquet garni* and liquidise the mixture in a blender or food processor, then push through a sieve and set aside.

Heat 2 tbsp oil in a pan. Put in the cumin seeds and, when they pop after a few seconds, add the remaining 3 cloves of peeled and sliced garlic and fry until light brown, then add to the liquidised tomato and pepper mixture. Add the sugar and salt to taste, re-heat and serve garnished with fresh coriander.

TANDOORI GRILLS

While the *tandoor*, an outdoor clay oven, originated in the old North West frontier, you can make a creditable tandoori dish under your grill or, even better, on a barbecue. Try it with this simple recipe.

tandoori grilled prawns
TANDOORI JHINGA

SERVES 4

12 raw king prawns, heads on
6–8 garlic cloves, chopped
1 tbsp chopped fresh ginger
1 heaped tsp garam masala powder (see page 19)
1 tbsp paprika powder
1 heaped tsp turmeric powder
Juice of ½ lemon
1 pinch of salt
3 tbsp vegetable oil
Slices of lime and chilli, to serve
A little salad (optional), to garnish

Shell and de-vein the prawns, leaving the heads on.

Process or pound together the garlic and ginger, adding a little water to make a paste. Add the remaining ingredients down to and including the oil, mix well and marinate the prawns in the mixture for a few minutes.

Heat a grill to maximum heat, thread the prawns on to 4 short skewers and arrange them in the position nearest to the heat. Grill until cooked, about 3 minutes, turning them over halfway. Serve with lime and chilli or mint and garnished, if you like, with a little salad.

tandoori grilled salmon
MACHLI GULNAAR

SERVES 4

500 g/1 lb 2 oz salmon fillet, skin left on, cut into chunks
  about 5 cm/2 in square

For the marinade
6–7 garlic cloves, peeled and finely chopped
4 cm/1¼ in length finger of ginger, peeled and chopped
2 tsp cumin powder
2 tsp paprika powder
1 tsp garam masala powder (see page 19)
1½ tsp turmeric powder
½ tsp red chilli powder
Juice of ½ lime
4–5 tbsp vegetable oil
Mint sauce (see page 132), to serve
Lime wedges, to garnish
Salt to taste

Process or pound together the garlic and ginger, adding a little water to make a paste. (Or use a blender or food processor to make a larger quantity, setting aside the remainder for a subsequent dish.)

Add the remaining ingredients, down to and including the oil, mix well and marinate the salmon chunks in the mixture for 1 to 2 hours.

Heat a grill to maximum, thread the salmon chunks on 4 skewers and arrange them in mid-position from the heat. Grill until cooked, about 4 to 5 minutes, turning them over at half time. Serve with the mint sauce and garnished with the lime wedges.

BELOW *Chef M.T. Ali, the stalwart of our tandoori ovens.*

A Porte des Indes creation. Buy the lobsters live and ask the fishmonger to split them lengthways into two, remove the stomach sacs and intestinal vein and trim off the feelers.

char-grilled lobster
LOBSTER ANARKALI

SERVES 4

2 lobsters, prepared by the fishmonger,
   as described above
¼ tsp red chilli powder
Salt to taste
Juice of ½ lemon
4–5 garlic cloves, peeled and finely chopped
2.5 cm/1 in length finger of ginger, peeled and
   finely chopped
3 tbsp thick yoghurt
2–3 stems fresh coriander, chopped
1 green chilli, chopped
½ tsp turmeric
A few strands of saffron warmed in 1 tbsp of milk
½ tsp ground white pepper
1 tsp garam masala powder (see page 19)
1 egg yolk
Melted butter, to baste
Tomato rougail (see page 135), to accompany

Wash the lobster halves under running water and pat dry with absorbent kitchen paper. Rub the red chilli powder and a little salt into the flesh. Sprinkle with the lemon juice and set aside.

Process or pound together the garlic and chopped ginger, adding a little water to make a paste. Put the yoghurt into a bowl with all the other ingredients except the butter, add the garlic and ginger paste and whisk thoroughly. Check seasoning and add salt to taste. Spread the mixture over the lobster meat.

Push two half lobsters on to each of two long skewers and arrange them under a grill in the medium position. Grill until done – about 6 to 8 minutes – turning and basting with a little melted butter. Serve with the tomato rougail.

Even without the traditional clay tandoori oven you can make an authentic version of this universally popular dish under a domestic grill. Or, even better, over a charcoal barbecue.

tandoori grilled chicken
MURGH TANDOORI

SERVES 4

1 whole chicken (free range if possible)
  or 2 chicken breasts and 2 legs, all skinned
1 tbsp lemon juice
1 tsp chilli powder
4 garlic cloves, peeled and chopped
1 heaped tbsp chopped fresh ginger
8–10 dried Kashmiri chillies, soaked in water for 1 hour
1 tsp cumin powder
1 tsp coriander powder
1 tbsp garam masala powder (see page 19)
240 ml/8 fl oz Greek yoghurt
1 tbsp vegetable oil
Salt to taste
A little salad, to garnish
Yoghurt and mint sauce (see page 132), to serve

If you are working with a whole chicken, divide it into 4 pieces; 2 legs and 2 breasts. Make light incisions diagonally on the outer surfaces of the flesh. Coat the chicken pieces with the lemon juice and chilli powder, rubbing it in with the fingers, and set aside for 15–20 minutes.

Pound, blend or process the garlic, ginger and chillies with a little water to make a paste and whisk it together with all the remaining ingredients except the salad and sauce. Add the chicken pieces and mix well to coat. Leave in the refrigerator overnight to marinate.

Heat the grill to maximum temperature and place the chicken pieces in the position nearest to the heat. Grill for 20 to 25 minutes, turning them over once. The meat should be charred a little. Garnish with a few salad leaves and serve with the yoghurt and mint sauce.

MEAT AND SEAFOOD

This rich seafood stew, reminiscent of a French *bouillabaise,* is a Pondicherry favourite, usually eaten with steamed rice. You can improvise your own mix of seafood according to what's available.

seafood stew
CASSOULET DE FRUITS DE MER

SERVES 4

500 g/1 lb 2 oz assortment of seafood: prawns,
    mussels, scallops, crab claws, squid and salmon
2 tbsp vegetable oil
1 sprig fresh curry leaves
½ Spanish onion, chopped
200 ml/7 fl oz coconut milk
2 tsp lemon juice
Salt to taste
Fresh coriander, to garnish
Steamed rice, to serve

For the paste
4 dry red chillies
2.5 cm/1 in length finger of ginger, peeled and chopped
3–4 garlic cloves, peeled and chopped
2 tsp coriander seeds
1 tsp cumin seeds
½ tsp turmeric
6 black peppercorns
1 tbsp malt vinegar

For the paste, pound or process all the ingredients together until they are homogenous.

Shell, trim and clean the seafood as required. Heat the oil in a pan and add the curry leaves followed by the chopped onion. Stir-fry until the onion is translucent, add the paste and sauté for 2 minutes.

Gently mix in the seafood except for the salmon and simmer for 2 minutes. Add the coconut milk, bring it to the boil, add the salmon, lower the heat and simmer until the fish is cooked, 5 to 7 minutes. Season with the lemon juice and salt to taste. Sprinkle with coriander leaves and serve hot with steamed rice.

This tiger prawn stir-fry is enlivened with fresh green garlic and spring onions. A seasonal dish, as fresh green garlic is only available in early Summer, though you can substitute ordinary garlic.

stir fried garlic prawns
LASOONI JHINGA

SERVES 4

16 tiger prawns, shelled, de-veined and heads removed
½ tsp salt
½ tsp turmeric powder
½ tsp red chilli powder
2 tbsp vegetable oil
5–6 fresh green garlic cloves, peeled and finely sliced
1 green chilli, seeded and cut into julienne (matchstick) strips
1 red chilli, seeded and cut into julienne (matchstick) strips
7 tbsp Kadai sauce (see page 131)
5 spring onions, including green part of stems, finely sliced
   or cut into julienne (matchstick) strips
Juice of ½ a lemon
Salt to taste

Rub the prawns with the salt, turmeric and chilli powders and set aside for at least 30 minutes.

Heat the oil in a pan, preferably a wok, and cook the garlic. When it is lightly browned, add the chillies and sauté for about 30 seconds. Toss in the prawns to sear for barely a minute, then add the Kadai sauce followed by the spring onions. Stir-fry over high heat for 1 minute. Add the lemon juice and salt to taste and serve hot.

Strips of mango give a cryptic edge to this coconut-rich Créole classic.

prawn and green mango curry
CREVETTES ASSADH

SERVES 4

2–3 tbsp vegetable oil
1 tsp mustard seeds
1 sprig curry leaves
½ medium Spanish onion, chopped
2 green chillies, seeded and cut into julienne
   (matchstick) strips
2–3 garlic cloves, peeled and pounded into a paste
   with a little water
½ tsp turmeric powder
400 ml/14 fl oz coconut milk
16 medium prawns, shelled and heads removed
½ medium green mango, flesh cut into julienne
   (matchstick) strips
Salt
Juice of ½ lime
Fried curry leaves, to garnish

Heat the oil, add the mustard seeds and cook for a few seconds until they splutter. Add the curry leaves followed by the chopped onion and green chillies. Sauté until the onion is translucent, then add the garlic paste and sauté for a further minute. Lower the heat and add the turmeric powder, followed by the coconut milk, prawns and mango julienne. Add salt to taste and cook gently for 3–4 minutes. Squeeze in the lime juice. Serve, garnished with fried curry leaves.

A typical Parsee prawn speciality, for
which every household has its own recipe.
This is Chef Mehernosh Mody's version.

parsee style prawns
KOLMI NO PATIO

SERVES 4

1 kg/2 lb 4 oz prawns, shelled and de-veined
Juice of 1 lime
1 tsp turmeric
Salt
1 knob tamarind, cut from the block
1 Spanish onion, finely sliced
3 tbsp vegetable oil
3 tbsp dhansak masala
4 medium tomatoes, finely chopped
4 drumstick vegetables*, peeled and cut into lengths of
    about 5 cm/2 in
Fresh coriander leaves, to garnish

For the paste
1 large Spanish onion, dry-roasted (see method)
7–8 dried Kashmiri chillies
2 tsp cumin seeds
3 tbsp coriander seeds
3 tsp poppy seeds
1.5 cm/½ in length cinnamon stick
4 cloves
2 green chillies, roughly chopped
A few stems fresh coriander, chopped
7 garlic cloves, roughly chopped

* Drumstick vegetables are the pods of moringa
oleifara *and are available fresh in Indian stores.*

Pre-heat oven to 240°C/465°F/Gas Mark 9.

Rub the lime juice, turmeric and salt into the prawns and set aside for at
least 30 minutes.

Soak the tamarind in hot water for 30 minutes, sieve and set aside the pulp.

For the paste, bake the large Spanish onion in the oven for about
10 minutes until the skin blackens, then remove, peel, discard the skin and
roughly chop the flesh. Dry-roast the Kashmiri chillies, cumin, coriander
and poppy seeds, cinnamon and cloves in a pan over medium heat for
about 1 minute, taking care not to burn them. Grind or process together
the dry-roasted mixture with the baked onion, chopped green chillies,
coriander and garlic, adding a little water to achieve a smooth consistency.

In a deep pan brown the sliced raw onion in the oil. Add the ground paste
and cook over medium heat for 5 to 6 minutes, then add the dhansak
masala and the tomatoes and cook and reduce for 8 to 10 minutes.

Meanwhile boil the peeled and cut drumsticks in water until tender, 10 to
15 minutes.

Add about 300 ml/10 fl oz water to the onion and paste mixture, return to
the boil and simmer for 7 to 10 minutes. Stir in the tamarind pulp, add the
prawns and simmer until they are done, about 5 to 7 minutes more. Toss in
the boiled drumsticks and check seasoning, adding more salt if necessary.
Serve garnished with fresh coriander leaves.

Madame Blanc, a *grande dame* of Pondicherry, contributed this stunning Créole recipe for marinated sea bass grilled in banana leaf. Best served with Tomato Rougail (see page 135). Kitchen foil can be substituted if necessary for the banana leaf in which the fish is wrapped.

sea bass baked in banana leaves
POLICHA MEEN

SERVES 4

2 wild sea bass weighing about 500 g/1 lb 2 oz each, scaled and gutted
½ tsp turmeric powder
½ tsp salt
Juice of 1 lemon
Banana leaf or foil, to wrap the fish
8 tbsp tomato rougail (see page 135), to serve
Sprigs of fresh green peppercorns and fresh red chillies cut into julienne (matchstick) strips, to garnish.

For the chutney
4 tbsp fresh green peppercorns, stripped from the stem
½ bunch fresh coriander
2 green chillies, seeded
5 garlic cloves, peeled
½ tsp cumin powder
Juice of ½ a lemon
Salt to taste

Cut 3 gashes on both sides of each fish, rub in the turmeric powder and salt and coat with the lemon juice. Set aside for at least 1 hour.

Grind or process all the chutney ingredients not too finely, incorporating the lemon juice and a pinch of salt. Smear the fish with the mixture, making sure it goes into the gashes and the inside cavity.

Pre-heat the oven to 180°C/350°F/Gas Mark 4. Parcel the fish in two pieces of banana leaf cut to the appropriate size and moistened with vegetable oil, securing the parcels with string or with toothpicks. (Or parcel the fish in oiled kitchen paper or foil.) Bake for 15 minutes.

Serve hot in the banana leaf with tomato rougail (see page 135) as an accompaniment and garnished with the green pepper and red chilli julienne.

Fish simmered in a creamy, mountain-herb curry of coconut, chillies, fresh coriander and roasted aromatic spices. Fillets of halibut or turbot may be substituted for the monkfish.

green fish curry
NILGIRI MACHI

SERVES 4

500 g/1 lb 2 oz monkfish tail
1/2 tsp turmeric powder
Salt to taste
3 tbsp vegetable oil
1/2 tsp mustard seeds
1 sprig curry leaves
1 Spanish onion, chopped
1 tsp coriander powder
1/2 tsp turmeric powder
1/2 tsp cumin powder
8 tbsp boiled onion sauce (see page 132)
5 tbsp coconut milk
Salt to taste
Fresh red chillies cut into julienne (matchstick) strips,
    to garnish

For the green curry paste
1 bunch coriander leaves
2–3 sprigs mint
2 green chillies, roughly chopped
2.5 cm/1 in finger of ginger, peeled and chopped
4–5 garlic cloves, peeled
Juice of 1/2 lemon

Rub the turmeric powder into the fish fillets with a little salt and set aside for at least half an hour. Meanwhile grind or process the green curry paste ingredients together, moistening with the lemon juice, to make a smooth paste.

Heat the oil in a pan and sauté the fish pieces on all sides for about 1 minute to seal. Lift out with a slotted spoon and set aside.

Put the mustard seeds into the same oil and, when they splutter after a few seconds, add the curry leaves followed by the chopped onion. Simmer gently until the onion is translucent, then add the spice powders and the boiled onion sauce. Stir well and simmer for 10 minutes.

Add the green curry paste and slowly return the mixture to a boil. Simmer for 5 minutes. Add the coconut milk and simmer for a further 4 to 5 minutes. Finally, return the fish and simmer until cooked, 7 to 8 minutes. Add salt to taste and serve garnished with a julienne of red chillies.

An ancestral recipe for this intriguingly
intense, sour and smoky dish which
comes from Sherin Mody's Kerala family.

kerala red fish curry
MEEN VAICH

SERVES 4

500 g/1 lb 2 oz monkfish tail or fillets of other fish,
    e.g. turbot, halibut or fresh cod
½ tsp salt
2 pieces kodampoli*
¼ tsp fenugreek seeds
1 tsp coriander seeds
3 tbsp Kashmiri red chilli powder
¼ tsp turmeric powder
3 tbsp vegetable oil
1 tsp mustard seeds
10–12 curry leaves
½ red onion, finely sliced
6–7 cloves garlic, peeled and thinly sliced
2.5 cm/1 in finger of ginger, peeled and thinly sliced
Idiappam (stringhoppers), to serve (see page 124)
Salt to taste

Wash the fish, pat dry with kitchen paper and cut into 12 pieces. Rub
with salt and set aside to marinate. Wash the kodampoli in 2 or 3 changes
of water and soak in 150 ml/5 fl oz warm water for at least 30 minutes.

Meanwhile, dry-roast the fenugreek and coriander seeds for a few seconds
in a frying pan, then grind. Be careful not to over-roast the seeds as this will
make them bitter. Mix this ground powder with the red chilli and turmeric
powders into 150 ml/5 fl oz water.

Heat the oil in a pan. Put in the mustard seeds and, when they pop after a
few seconds, add the curry leaves, onion, garlic and ginger and fry until the
onion is translucent, 3 to 4 minutes.

Stir in the powdered spices in their water and cook for 3 to 4 minutes, then
add a further 350 ml/11 fl oz water and simmer for 20 minutes.

Add the soaked kadampuli with its water and salt to taste. Continue to
simmer until the mixture thickens a little, about 10 to 12 minutes, then add
the fish pieces and gently simmer for 10 to 12 minutes until the fish is
cooked. Be careful not to overcook. Serve with Idiappam (see page 124).

* Kodampoli is a local Kerala dried fruit similar to tamarind found in South Indian
shops. There is no really suitable substitute but use tamarind if necessary.

roasted duck breasts in a spicy tamarind sauce

MAGRET DE CANARD PULIVAAR

A unique Créole dish of duck breasts
cooked in a rare blend of spices.
Madame Lourdes Swamy of Pondicherry
supplied the recipe.

SERVES 4

4 unskinned Barbary duck breast fillets

For the marinade
1 tsp black pepper powder
1 tsp coriander powder
½ tsp cumin powder
½ tsp red chilli powder
½ tsp turmeric powder
2 tbsp vegetable oil
1 tbsp malt vinegar
1 pinch fenugreek

For the sauce
2 tbsp coriander seeds
4 tsp cumin seeds
1 pinch fenugreek seeds
1 tsp black peppercorns
1 tsp whole cloves
2.5 cm/1 in length cinnamon stick
30 g/1 oz vadavam (see page 21)
5 dried red chillies
60 g/2 oz desiccated coconut
150 ml/5 fl oz onion sauce (see page 132)
3 tbsp tomato paste
4 tbsp tamarind pulp

To finish
2 tbsp vegetable oil
1 tsp mustard seeds
10–12 curry leaves
Sprigs of fresh green peppercorns, julienne strips of fresh red
    chillies, fried coconut chips (optional), to garnish

Prick the duck breasts in several places with the tines of a fork. Mix the marinade ingredients together and rub into the breasts. Set aside for at least half an hour, then pre-heat the oven to 180°C/350°F/Gas Mark 4.

Meanwhile, dry-roast separately over a medium heat each of the spice ingredients for the sauce, stirring continuously until the aroma is released, about 1 minute. Roast the desiccated coconut until light brown. Grind or process together all the roasted ingredients, adding a little water, to make a fine paste. Mix the paste with the onion sauce and tomato paste in a pan and bring to the boil, stirring continuously. Simmer for 20 minutes, stirring occasionally to prevent sticking, then add the tamarind pulp.

To finish, heat the oil in another pan, add the mustard seeds and the curry leaves and, in a few seconds, as soon as the mustard seeds pop, stir into the sauce and add salt to taste.

Arrange the duck breasts skin side down in an oiled roasting tin and roast for 10 to 12 minutes to cook the flesh pink, 18–20 minutes for well done. Remove from the oven and cut breasts into narrow diagonal slices. Fan out on heated plates and pour over the sauce. Garnish with sprigs of fresh green peppercorns, fresh red chilli juliennes and fried coconut chips. (Or use dehydrated coconut chips, dry-roasted until they're light brown.)

This mild and sinfully rich dish is a long-standing favourite at La Porte des Indes. It's also surprisingly easy to prepare.

chicken in a creamy red sauce
POULET ROUGE

SERVES 4

4 legs cooked tandoori chicken
5 garlic cloves, peeled and chopped
25 g/1 oz butter
2 tbsp tandoori masala powder
5 tbsp yoghurt
200 ml/7 fl oz onion sauce (see page 132)
200 ml/7 fl oz double cream
Salt to taste

Cut the flesh from the cooked chicken to shreds, discarding bones.

Crush the garlic in a mortar with a little water to make a paste. Melt the butter in a pan and lightly brown the garlic paste in it. Add the tandoori masala powder and sauté for a few seconds before lowering the heat and adding the yoghurt. Stir the mixture for 1–2 minutes and add the onion sauce, mix well, add the cream, bring the mixture back to the boil and simmer for 10 minutes.

Add the shredded chicken flesh and continue to simmer for 2 to 3 minutes until the meat is heated through. Add salt to taste and serve hot.

This mild, coconut-flavoured dish comes from the old Syrian Christian missionary community of Kerala. Sherin Mody learned the recipe from her mother. Kerala chicken stew is best eaten with Pain Créole (see page 126).

kerala chicken stew
KOZHI ISTEW

SERVES 4

1 chicken weighing about 1.5 kg/3 lb 5 oz,
   cut into 8 pieces
Salt
4 tbsp vegetable oil
5 cm/2 in length cinnamon stick
6–7 black peppercorns
2–3 cloves
12 curry leaves
200 g/7 oz shallots, chopped
4 cm/1½ in finger of ginger, peeled and cut into julienne
   (matchstick) strips
2 fresh green chillies, finely chopped
200 g potatoes, peeled and cut into 2.5 cm/1 in cubes
600 ml/1 pint thick coconut milk
1 tbsp rice flour
1 tsp garam masala powder (see page 19)
Pain Créole (see page 126), to serve

Wash the chicken pieces, pat dry with kitchen paper and rub in salt.

Heat the oil in a pan and put in the cinnamon, peppercorns, cloves and curry leaves. After a few seconds add the shallots and fry until they are translucent, about 2 to 3 minutes, then add the ginger and chopped chillies. Add the chicken pieces and the potatoes and sear on each side over high heat.

Reduce the heat and add 300 ml/½ pint water, return to the boil and simmer for 8 minutes. Add the coconut milk (shaking well before opening cans), bring to the boil and simmer for 5 minutes. Add the rice flour mixed with 2 tbsp of water and the garam masala powder, return to the boil and simmer gently for another 5–7 minutes until the chicken pieces are cooked through. Add salt to taste.

This country-style recipe is a favourite of Bobby Singh, chef at Brussels Porte des Indes. It comes from his native Punjab.

chicken patiala-style
PATIALA DHABA MURG

SERVES 4

30 g/1 oz cashew nuts, skinned
50 g/1½ oz melon seeds
4 tsp poppy seeds
7 garlic cloves, peeled and finely chopped
5 cm/2 in length finger of ginger, peeled and finely chopped
1 tsp lemon juice
1½ tsp turmeric powder
1 chicken, cut into 8 pieces
3 tbsp vegetable oil
3 cardamom pods
2 cloves
2.5 cm/1 in length cinnamon stick
2 bay leaves
200 g/7 oz Spanish onion, chopped
3–4 fresh green chillies, chopped
1 tsp coriander powder
200 g/7 oz tomatoes, chopped
1 tsp garam masala powder (see page 19)
Salt to taste
Chopped fresh coriander and fried cashew nut halves, to garnish

Soak the cashew nuts, melon and poppy seeds in water for 1 hour and grind or process with the soaking water to a smooth paste.

Take half the chopped garlic and half the ginger and pound with a little water to make a smooth paste. Add the lemon juice and ½ tsp turmeric powder to the garlic and ginger paste and smear the mixture over the chicken pieces. Marinate for 30 minutes.

Make a separate paste with the remainder of the garlic and set aside.

Heat the oil in a pan, put in the cardamom pods, cloves, cinnamon and bay leaves and after a few seconds add the chopped onions and fry until they are a light golden brown. Add the reserved garlic paste and cook for a further 2 minutes, then add the remaining chopped ginger, the green chillies, the remaining turmeric powder, coriander powder and the chopped tomatoes. Cook until the tomatoes soften, about 5 minutes.

Add the nut and seed paste and cook over low heat, stirring continuously to prevent sticking for about 10–12 minutes until oil appears on the surface. Add the chicken pieces and a little water, cover and cook until the chicken is done, about 20 minutes. Adjust the salt, stir in the garam masala powder and serve garnished with the coriander and cashew nut halves.

The idea of putting grilled chicken tikka cubes into a masala sauce may have originated in Britain. Be that as it may, with its turmeric-coloured golden yellow sauce, this is the Porte des Indes unique version.

chicken tikka masala

SERVES 4

2 tbsp vegetable ghee
½ tsp cumin seeds
2 fresh green chillies, finely chopped
3 garlic cloves, peeled and finely chopped
2.5 cm/1 in length finger of ginger, peeled and finely chopped
1 tsp coriander powder
½ tsp turmeric powder
7 tbsp natural yoghurt
5 tbsp onion sauce (see page 132)
30 g/1 oz paneer, grated
400 g/14 oz cooked chicken tikka pieces (see page 42)
6 tbsp double cream
1 tsp garam masala powder
Salt to taste
Fresh coriander, to garnish

Heat the ghee, put in the cumin seeds and, after a few seconds when they crackle and pop, add the green chillies, garlic and ginger. Sauté until light brown, about 3 minutes, then lower the heat and add the coriander and turmeric powders and cook, stirring, for 1 minute.

Add the yoghurt, the onion sauce, the grated paneer or cottage cheese and, finally, the chicken tikka pieces. Stir and cook for 2 minutes, add the cream and garam masala powder and simmer for 2 minutes more. Add salt to taste and serve hot, garnished with fresh coriander.

A special, freshly dry-roasted masala and stir-frying give this dish its unique savour. This dish is contributed by our Chef Anand Singh Negi, who hails from Dehradun.

chettinad guinea fowl
KATH KOZHI CHETTINAD

SERVES 4

4 boned guinea fowl breasts
Salt
2 pinches turmeric
2 garlic cloves, peeled
1.25 cm/½ in length fresh ginger
Juice of ½ lemon
2 tbsp vegetable oil
½ tsp mustard seeds
1 sprig curry leaves
1 medium red onion, chopped
1 medium tomato, chopped
½ lemon
Squeeze of lime juice

For the chettinad masala
2 tsp black peppercorns
6 cloves
1.25 cm/½ in cinnamon stick
2 tsp coriander seeds
½ tsp fenugreek seeds
1 tsp fennel seeds
1 tsp dried grated coconut
2 whole red chillies
6–8 curry leaves

Dry-roast the chettinad ingredients individually in a heavy-based pan until they are medium brown. Grind them together and mix with a little water to make a paste. Set aside.

Cut the guinea fowl breasts into thin strips, rub in a little salt and the turmeric. Chop the garlic and ginger finely, and pound to a smooth paste, adding a little water. Rub this into the chicken strips, followed by the lemon juice. Set the breasts aside for 30 minutes to marinate.

Heat the oil in a pan. Add the mustard seeds and, after a few seconds when they pop, add the curry leaves, then the onion and fry until golden brown. Add the chettinad masala and simmer for 2 minutes. Add the chopped tomato and cook a further 2 minutes, then put in the strips of guinea fowl and toss and stir-fry until done, about 2 minutes. Adjust seasoning and squeeze lime juice over.

The five spices used in this Lucknow recipe are the same as those used in pickling, which is what gives this freshly prepared dish a striking flavour.

rabbit in pickling spices
ACHARI KHARGOSH

SERVES 4

2.5 cm/1 in length finger of ginger, peeled and
    finely chopped
3 garlic cloves, peeled and finely chopped
125 ml/4 fl oz thick yoghurt
Salt to taste
500 g/1 lb 2 oz boned rabbit, cut into bite-sized cubes
30 g/1 oz cashew nuts
2 fresh green chillies
2 fresh red chillies
3 tbsp vegetable oil
1 cardamom pod
1 clove
1 cm/¼ in length cinnamon stick
200 g/7 oz Spanish onion, sliced
2 tsp white vinegar
1 tsp garam masala powder (see page 19)
Chopped fresh coriander, to garnish

For the pickling spices
1½ tsp cumin seeds
1 tsp onion seeds
1 tsp fennel seeds
1 tsp mustard seeds
½ tsp fenugreek seeds

Pound the pickling spices coarsely and set aside. Pound the ginger and garlic together with a little water to make a smooth paste. Mix this with the yoghurt, add salt to taste and stir in the cubed rabbit. Leave to marinate for at least 3 hours.

Soak the cashew nuts in water for 1 hour, then drain and grind or process into a smooth paste. Slit open the green and red chillies lengthways and stuff with some of the pounded pickling spices, reserving the remainder.

Heat the oil in a pan and put in the cardamom, clove and cinnamon, then add the sliced onion and fry until it is translucent. Remove the meat from the marinade, put it into the pan with the onions and sear on all sides. Whisk the marinade smooth and add, stirring continuously to prevent the yoghurt curdling. Bring to the boil and simmer for 10–12 minutes. Add the cashew nut paste and salt to taste and, continuing to stir to prevent the paste from sticking to the bottom of the pan, simmer for a few minutes more.

Heat a little oil in another pan and sauté the stuffed chillies and remaining pickling spices for 1 to 2 minutes, tossing to prevent them burning. Add the vinegar and tip into the pan containing the meat. Add the garam masala powder, stir well and cover the pan with a tight-filling lid.

Cook over a medium heat for 10 to 12 minutes. Serve garnished with chopped coriander.

This is the recipe of young Chef Francisco Marques, a true Goan. It was once dubbed 'ordinaire' by London restaurant critic Fay Maschler. You may not agree!

goan pork curry
PORK VINDALOO 'ORDINAIRE'

SERVES 4

400 g/14 oz leg of pork
200 g/7 oz belly of pork
½ tsp turmeric powder
½ tsp red chilli powder
3 tbsp vegetable oil
3 bay leaves
250 g/8 oz Spanish onions, finely sliced
2 tbsp tomato paste
10–12 cocktail onions
Salt to taste
Red chillies, fried, to garnish

Paste for the sauce
12–15 dried red Kashmiri chillies
2 tsp cumin seeds
4 tsp coriander seeds
½ tsp black peppercorns
3 cloves
4 cm/1¾ in length cinnamon stick
2 cardamom pods
4 cm/1¾ in finger of ginger, peeled and finely chopped
6 garlic cloves, peeled and finely chopped
3 tbsp malt vinegar

Cut the pork into bite-sized cubes. Mix the turmeric with the chilli powder and rub into the meat with your fingers. Set aside for at least two hours or, preferably, overnight. Soak the sauce ingredients in the malt vinegar for 1 hour and grind or process into a smooth paste.

Heat the oil in a pan. Put in the bay leaves and the onion and fry until the onion is a very light golden brown. Add the paste for the sauce and fry for 3 to 4 minutes, then add the marinated pork, the tomato paste and a little water to prevent sticking. Cook over medium heat until the meat is well done, about 25 minutes. Add the cocktail onions and salt to taste and serve garnished with the fried red chillies.

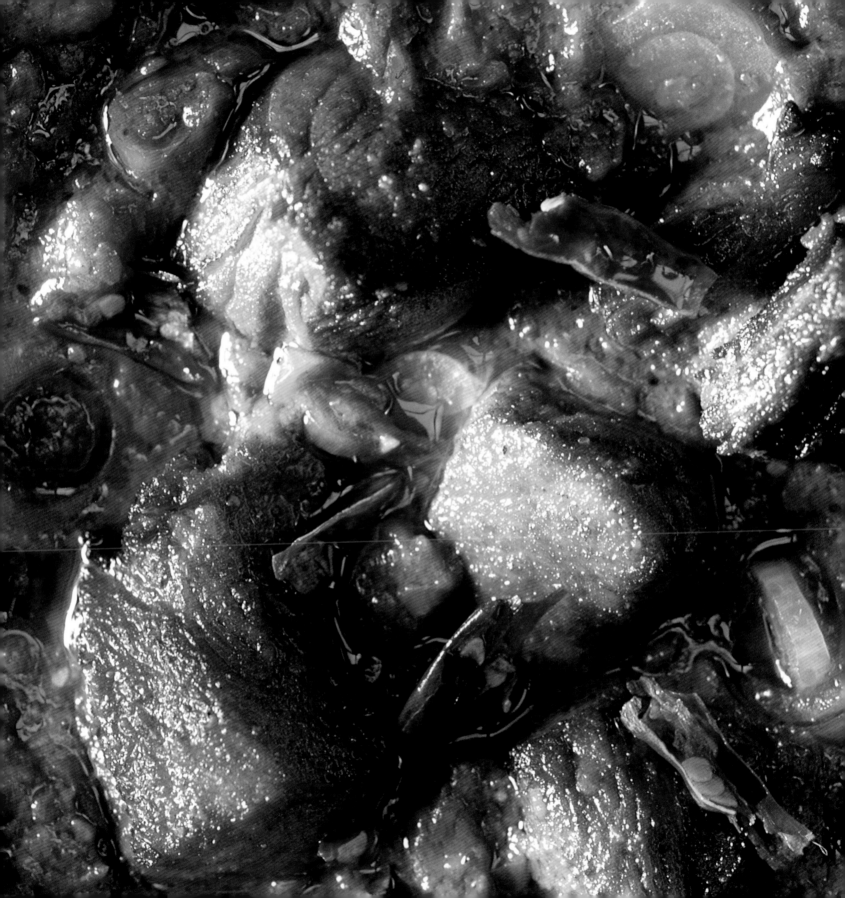

This spicy pork recipe comes from the small, hilly Coorgi region on India's south-west coast.

southern indian pork curry
COORGI PANDHI KARI

SERVES 4

350 g/12 oz pork loin, cut into 2.5cm/1 in cubes
150 g/5 oz pork belly, cut into 2.5 cm/1 in cubes
Salt
1 tsp turmeric powder
3 green cardamom pods
5 cloves
1.5 cm/½ in length cinnamon
1 tsp coriander seeds
½ tsp cumin seeds
½ tsp mustard seeds
½ tsp black peppercorns
3 tbsp vegetable oil
2 Spanish onions, sliced
4 green chillies, finely chopped
5 cm/2 in length finger of ginger, peeled and finely chopped
6 garlic cloves, peeled and finely chopped
Leaves of 1 bunch fresh coriander, chopped
3 tbsp Kachampuli vinegar*
Dried red chillies, fried, to garnish

Rub the meat with salt and turmeric powder and set aside.

Dry roast the cardamom pods, cloves, cinnamon, coriander seeds, cumin seeds, mustard seeds and black peppercorns for about 1 minute over medium heat, shaking the pan gently and taking care that they do not char. Remove them from the heat and grind them together into a fine powder.

Heat the oil and gently fry the sliced onions over low heat until they are translucent. Add the chopped green chillies, ginger and garlic and cook for a further 4 to 5 minutes. Increase the heat to high and put in the meat, turning it to seal it on all sides. Lower the heat, add the roasted and ground spices and a little water, cover and simmer for 20 to 30 minutes until the meat is nearly cooked. Do not add too much water as the sauce should have a thick consistency.

Meanwhile blend or process the coriander leaves into a purée. Add the Kachampuli vinegar, the coriander purée to the meat pan and salt to taste. Simmer for 8 to 10 minutes more and serve hot, garnished with the fried dried red chillies.

*Kachampuli vinegar comes from the Coorgi region. If you can't find it in a South Indian shop, substitute 2 parts brown malt vinegar mixed with 1 part balsamic vinegar.

Based on a treasured recipe from the royal kitchens of the
Nizam of Hyderabad, Chef Anand's ingenious version tastes
even better when done on a charcoal barbecue.

barra lamb chops
ADRAK KE PANJE

SERVES 4

8 or 12 lamb chops, according to size

For the tandoori paste
2 garlic cloves, peeled and finely chopped
1.25cm/$\frac{1}{2}$ in length fresh ginger, finely chopped
2 Spanish onions, sliced
3 tbsp vegetable oil
Juice of $\frac{1}{2}$ lemon
1 green chilli, seeded and finely chopped
1 tsp turmeric
$\frac{1}{2}$ tsp garam masala powder (see page 19)
$\frac{1}{2}$ tsp chilli powder
$\frac{1}{2}$ tsp cardamom powder
$\frac{1}{2}$ tsp ground mace
Salt to taste

Process or pound together the garlic and ginger, adding a little water to make a smooth paste. (You may find it practical to make this paste in larger quantities and store the surplus in a jar with a tight-fitting lid in the refrigerator for subsequent use.) Set aside.

Fry the sliced onions in a little of the vegetable oil until they are brown. Mix or process with a little water to a smooth paste. Set aside.

Beat the lamb chops lightly with a cooking mallet to flatten them slightly.

Whisk the garlic and ginger into the browned onion paste and mix in all the remaining ingredients. Add the chops and mix well to coat them. Cover and refrigerate overnight to marinate.

Heat a grill to maximum temperature and arrange the chops in the position nearest to the heat source. If you like your meat to be pink, grill the chops for 3 to 4 minutes, turning them over once. If you prefer them well done, grill for 6 to 8 minutes.

It's essential to follow the method described if you are going to reproduce all the savour of this great classic dish.

lamb biryani
HYDERABADI BIRYANI

SERVES 4

1 kg/2 lb 4 oz boned leg of lamb, cut into 2.5 cm/1 in cubes
3 tbsp vegetable ghee
500 ml/18 fl oz meat bouillon
1 tbsp cream
Juice of ½ lemon
1 tsp cardamom powder
1 tsp mace powder
2 tomatoes, diced
2.5 cm/1 in length finger of ginger cut into julienne (fine matchstick) strips
2 green chillies, cut similarly to the ginger
A few strands saffron, soaked in milk
A knob of butter, cut into dice
Vegetable raita (see page 131), to serve

For the marinade
½ Spanish onion, sliced
2 tbsp vegetable oil
2.5 cm/1 in length finger of ginger, peeled and finely chopped
4 garlic cloves, peeled and finely chopped
2 cloves
3 cardamom pods
2 bay leaves
2.5 cm/1 in length cinnamon stick
1 tsp black cumin seeds
1 tsp red chilli powder
1 tsp turmeric powder
4 tbsp yoghurt

For the rice
500g/1lb 2 oz Basmati rice
1 tsp coriander seeds
1 tsp black cumin seeds
2 cloves
3 cardamom pods
2.5 cm/1 in length cinnamon stick

For the marinade, fry the onion in vegetable oil until brown. Pound the chopped ginger and garlic in a mortar with a little water to make a paste. Dry-roast the cloves, cardamom pods, bay leaves and cinnamon, grind them together into a powder and mix with all the marinade ingredients. Coat the cubed lamb with the marinade and set aside for 1 hour.

In a thick copper-bottomed saucepan or ironware pot, heat the vegetable ghee and seal the lamb cubes on all sides over high heat. Lower the heat and cook gently for 10 minutes, stirring to prevent sticking. Add enough meat bouillon to barely cover the lamb cubes and cook over medium heat until almost done, about 40 minutes, stirring occasionally and allowing the bouillon to reduce to a thickish consistency.

Meanwhile rinse the rice in a sieve under running water and drain. Cut a square of muslin large enough to contain the spices for the rice, put them into it and tie with thread. Put cold water equal to twice the volume of the rice into a saucepan with this spice bag and bring to the boil, add salt and put in the rice. Return to the boil and simmer for 8 to 10 minutes, then remove the spice bag and drain the rice.

Preheat oven to 180°C/350°F/Gas Mark 4.

Lower the heat under the lamb and stir in the cream, lemon juice, cardamom and mace powders, diced tomatoes, the ginger and chilli julienne strips and half the saffron. Spread the rice in an even layer over the meat. Drizzle over the remaining saffron in its milk and dot with the butter. Cover the saucepan with a damp muslin cloth or with kitchen foil and a lid to seal in moisture and cook in the oven for 12 to 15 minutes. Alternatively, finish the cooking on the stove over a very gentle heat.

This version of the classic lamb curry of Kashmir delivers a rich succulence without a heavy dose of cholesterol. The recipe is contributed by Chef Ramesh Chand, a master of curries and biryanis, who honed his skills with veteran North Indian chefs in Delhi.

lamb shanks with saffron
ROGANJOSH

SERVES 4

500 g/1 lb red onions, sliced
1 tbsp vegetable oil
15 g/½ oz fresh ginger, peeled and finely chopped
3–4 garlic cloves, peeled and finely chopped
75 g/3 oz vegetable ghee
2.5 cm/1 in length cinnamon stick
850 g/2 lb lamb shanks, cut into 6 cm/2½ in cubes including bone
1 tbsp coriander powder
1 tsp Kashmiri chilli powder
200 g/7 oz tomatoes, chopped
3 tbsp natural yoghurt
½ tsp garam masala (see page 19)
12–15 strands saffron
½ tsp fennel powder
Salt to taste
Fresh coriander, chopped and cherry tomatoes, to garnish (optional)

Fry the sliced onions in the oil until they are brown. Pound or process with a little water to make a smooth paste. Pound or process together the ginger and garlic with a little water to make a second paste. Set aside both pastes.

Heat the ghee, put in the cinnamon and sauté for 10 to 15 seconds. Add the ginger and garlic paste and brown. Add the cubed lamb shanks and seal over high heat for about 4 minutes, making sure that the cubes are browned on all sides. Lower the heat and add the coriander and chilli powders and, 1 minute later, the chopped tomatoes. Simmer for 5 minutes and then add the yoghurt and simmer for a further 3 minutes.

Add the onion paste, return to the boil and simmer for 20 minutes, adding water if required to maintain a moist consistency. Add the garam masala, saffron stands, fennel powder and salt and cook for a further 5 minutes. Serve scattered with coriander leaves and, if you like, garnished with cherry tomatoes.

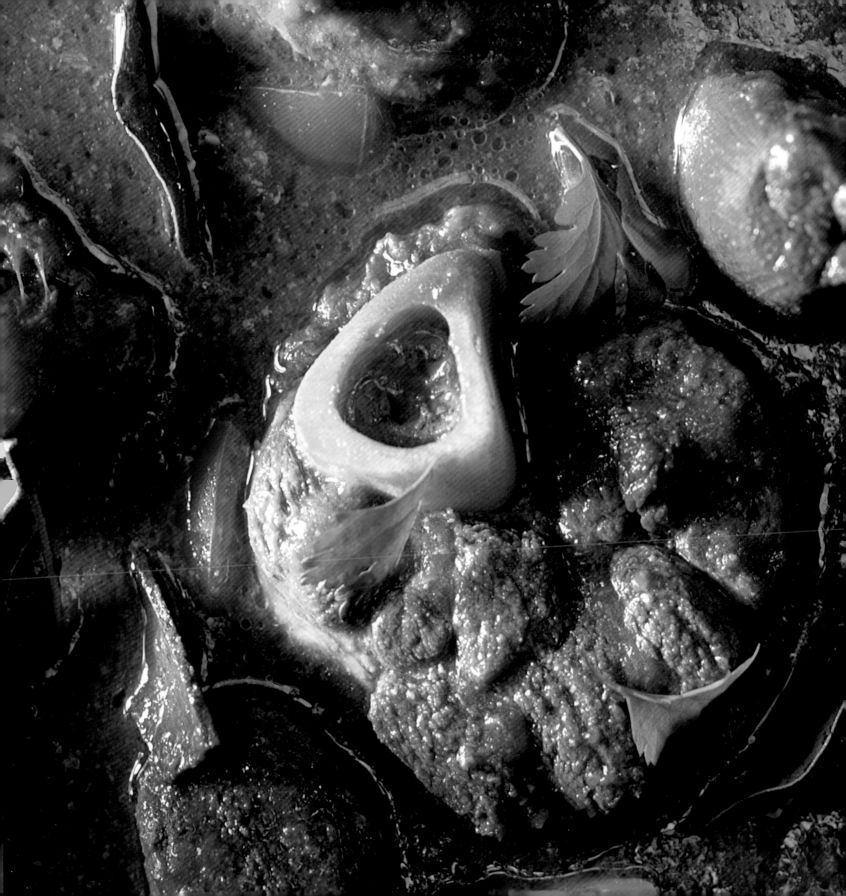

This stir-fried beef dish comes from Karaikal, a small ex-French enclave south of Pondicherry.

stir fried beef with coconut
CHUMUDE KARAIKAL

SERVES 4

1 tsp chilli powder
½ tsp turmeric powder
Salt to taste
2 tbsp vegetable oil
300 g/10½ oz beef rump cut into thin slices about
    2.5 cm/1 in square
10 curry leaves
3 whole dried red chillies
30 g/1 oz fresh or dehydrated coconut chips
    (dry-roasted if fresh)
2 medium tomatoes, finely chopped

For the spice mix
½ tsp coriander seeds
½ tsp cumin seeds
5 black peppercorns
1 pinch fenugreek seeds
1 pinch aniseed
½ pod star anise
0.5 cm/⅕ in length cinnamon stick

Mix the chilli powder, turmeric and salt with 1 tbsp vegetable oil and rub the mixture into the beef slices. Set aside.

Dry-roast the spice mix ingredients together over medium heat for 1 minute, taking care that they do not burn, then grind them to a fine powder.

Heat the remaining vegetable oil in a wok or deep-frying pan and put in the curry leaves and the dried red chillies each torn into 2 or 3 pieces. Add the beef and the coconut chips, retaining a few of the latter for garnish, and sauté over high heat until the meat is seared on both sides. Reduce the heat and add the chopped tomatoes, the ground spices and salt to taste. Stir-fry until the meat is done, about 2 to 3 minutes. Serve hot, garnished with the remaining coconut chips.

VEGETABLES

Grilling the aubergines helps to give a unique flavour to this classic Créole recipe, especially if, as in Pondicherry, you do it over live charcoal.

smoked aubergine crush
ROUGAIL D'AUBERGINE

SERVES 4

4 medium aubergines, weighing about 500 g/1 lb 2 oz in all
2 tbsp vegetable oil
½ tsp mustard seeds
1 Spanish onion, chopped
4 cm/1¾ in length finger of ginger, peeled and finely chopped
1 fresh red chilli, finely chopped
1 fresh green chilli, finely chopped
½ tsp turmeric powder
4 tbsp coconut milk
2 tsp lemon juice
Salt to taste
Fresh coriander, chopped and fresh red chillies cut into julienne (matchstick) strips, to garnish

Pre-heat the oven to 200°C/400°F/Gas Mark 6. Prick the aubergines on each side with the tines of a fork and smear with a little oil. Cook for 20 minutes in the oven (or over charcoal) until done. Remove from the heat and, when they are cool enough to handle, halve lengthways, scoop out the flesh and blend or process it to a purée.

Heat the oil in a saucepan, put in the mustard seeds and, when they splutter after a few seconds, add the chopped onions and fry until they are translucent. Then add the ginger, the red and green chillies and sauté for 2 minutes.

Lower the heat and add the turmeric followed by the puréed aubergine. Cook, stirring, over a low heat for 15 minutes, then add the coconut milk and stir for a further 2 minutes. Add the lemon juice and salt to taste. Serve hot, garnished with the fresh coriander and red chillies.

The flavour of okra or ladies' fingers is best brought out by adding them last to a subtly spiced tomato mixture.

stir fried okra with onions
NAINTARA DO PYAZ

SERVES 4

2 tbsp vegetable oil
1 tsp cumin seeds
1 Spanish onion, diced
4 cm/1¾ in long finger of fresh ginger, finely chopped
3–4 green chillies, finely chopped
2 medium tomatoes, seeded and diced into 1cm/¼ in cubes
½ tsp turmeric powder
½ tsp red chilli powder
400 g/13 oz okra (ladies' fingers) cut into 1 cm/¼ in lengths
3 tsp lemon juice
2 tsp chaat masala
A few stems fresh coriander, chopped
Fresh coriander and cherry tomatoes (optional), to garnish
Salt to taste

Heat the oil in a pan, put in the cumin seeds and, when they splutter after a few seconds, add half the diced onion and cook until translucent. Add the ginger and green chillies and brown lightly, then toss in half the diced tomatoes and stir-fry for 2 minutes. Stir in the turmeric and red chilli powders, add the okra and cook for 2 to 3 minutes. Add remaining onion and tomato and cook for a further 2 minutes. Add the lemon juice, chaat masala and chopped coriander and serve hot with more fresh coriander and, if you like, cherry tomatoes, to garnish.

Large, mild green chillies in a spicy and nutty coconut sauce.

Chef Sundeep Bhagat from Lucknow, our specialist in vegetarian cuisine, contributed this recipe.

mild chillies in a nutty sauce
MIRCHI KA SALAN

SERVES 4

8 large green chillies (about 15–20 cm/6–8 in long)
4 tbsp vegetable oil
1 tsp turmeric
5 tbsp onion sauce (see page 132)
60 g/2 oz tomatoes, chopped
½ tsp red chilli powder
Salt to taste
8 tbsp yoghurt
½ tsp mustard seeds
2 sprigs curry leaves
½ tsp lemon juice
Fried dried red chillies, to garnish

For the sauce
Flesh of ½ coconut, grated*
30 g/1 oz peanuts
15 g/½ oz cashew nuts
2 tsp sesame seeds
1 tsp coriander seeds
½ tsp black peppercorns
½ tsp fennel seeds
1 small piece dried tamarind, about 1 heaped tsp
  in volume, soaked in water

Slit the green chillies lengthways along one side and set aside. Lightly dry-roast all the sauce ingredients in a frying pan and grind or process them with a little water to make a smooth paste. Set aside.

Heat 2 tbsp of the oil in a pan, put in the turmeric powder and the onion sauce and heat gently. Add the chopped tomatoes, red chilli powder and salt. Whisk the yoghurt and stir into the mixture. Continue to stir until the mixture thickens, 5 to 6 minutes. Add the sauce paste and continue to cook until oil rises to the surface, 10 to 12 minutes.

In another pan heat remaining oil and lightly sauté the green chillies for 2 to 3 minutes, then lift out and add to the yoghurt mixture. Now put the mustard seeds and curry leaves into the oil and, when the mustard seeds pop after a few seconds, stir both ingredients with the cooking oil into the sauce. If sauce is too thick, thin with some water. Taste and check if more salt is needed, stir in the lemon juice and serve garnished with the fried red chillies.

* There is no substitute for fresh grated coconut. Chop a coconut in two with a cleaver and remove the flesh by sliding a sharp knife between it and the hard shell. Then grate it with a coarse grater. The unused coconut flesh may be kept in the refrigerator or deep-frozen and used for a subsequent dish.

spinach and cheese
SAAG PANEER

SERVES 4

1 kg/2 lb 2 oz fresh spinach, washed and roughly chopped
2 tbsp vegetable oil
1 level tsp cumin seeds
1 Spanish onion, chopped
4–5 garlic cloves, peeled and finely chopped
2.5 cm/1 in length finger of ginger, peeled and finely chopped
2 green chillies, chopped
2 tsp dried fenugreek leaves
1 large or 2 small tomatoes, chopped
150 g/5 oz paneer, cut into 1 cm/¼ in cubes
Oil for deep-frying
1 knob butter
2–3 tbsp thick cream
Salt to taste

Plunge the spinach into boiling water and blanch for 30 seconds. Drain and gently press out excess liquid. Set aside.

Heat 2 tbsp of oil and put in the cumin seeds. When they pop after a few seconds add the onion and cook until translucent, then add the garlic and ginger and fry for 1 to 2 minutes. Add the chillies and dried fenugreek leaves and cook for a further minute. Add the tomatoes and cook for 5 to 7 minutes before mixing in the spinach and cooking for another 5 minutes over a low heat.

Meanwhile deep-fry the paneer cubes in oil heated to 160°C/320°F until the edges are light brown, about 1 minute. Add the paneer cubes to the spinach and stir in the butter, cream and salt to taste.

bombay style potatoes
BOMBAY ALOO

SERVES 4

500 g/1 lb 2 oz baby new potatoes
2 tbsp vegetable oil
1 tsp cumin seeds
3–4 garlic cloves, peeled and finely chopped
2.5 cm/1 in length finger of ginger, peeled and finely chopped
3–4 green chillies, finely chopped
½ tsp turmeric powder
Salt to taste
5–6 tbsp Kadai sauce (see page 131)
A few stems fresh coriander
1 knob butter
½ fresh lime
Cherry tomatoes and more fresh coriander, to garnish (optional)

Put the potatoes into boiling water and boil for 15 minutes. Drain, and when they are cool enough to handle, cut in half.

Heat the oil in a saucepan, put in the cumin seeds and, after a few seconds, add the finely chopped garlic, ginger and green chillies and fry until they are lightly browned. Then add the turmeric and salt.

Toss in the potatoes and stir-fry for 1 minute, then add the Kadai sauce, the fresh coriander and butter and stir-fry to mix, squeezing in the lime juice.

Serve hot, garnished, if you like, with cherry tomatoes and more fresh coriander. This dish also makes a good accompaniment to any meat curry.

Subtly spice-tempered red and yellow lentils make an ideal

foil for all richly flavoured dishes.

tempered yellow lentils
TADKA DAL

SERVES 4 AS AN ACCOMPANIMENT

100 g/3½ oz masoor dal (red lentils)
60 g/2 oz toor dal (yellow lentils)
3 tbsp vegetable oil
1 heaped tsp cumin seeds
1 medium red onion, chopped
7 garlic cloves, peeled and finely sliced
1 fresh green chilli, finely chopped
1 large tomato, chopped
1 tsp chilli powder
½ tsp turmeric powder
Fresh coriander, to garnish
Salt to taste

Put both kinds of lentil into a saucepan, cover with cold water (about 1.5 litres/2½ pints), bring to the boil and boil gently until they are soft, about 30 to 35 minutes.

In a frying pan, heat the oil very hot, put in the cumin seeds and, when they splutter a few seconds later, add the chopped onion and brown lightly. Add the garlic and fry until it is also light brown, then add the chopped chilli and fry for a few seconds before adding the chopped tomato, followed by the powdered spices. Simmer for 7 to 8 minutes.

Add the mixture to the boiled lentils and mix well. Return to the boil and simmer for 10 to 15 minutes. Serve hot, garnished with fresh coriander.

Earthy brown chestnut mushrooms in a green herb sauce. A vegetarian version of a classic dish from the Coorg mountains of South India. Contributed by Chef Rohit Kumar, one of the young chefs in the brigade, who excels in regional cuisine.

coorgi mushroom curry

SERVES 4

1 tbsp vegetable oil
200 g/ 7 oz red onion, roughly chopped
2 fresh green chillies, roughly chopped
1 small sliver of ginger, chopped
1 garlic clove, peeled and chopped
1 pinch turmeric powder
2 tbsp malt vinegar
90 g/3 oz fresh coriander leaves, roughly chopped
4 tbsp water
150 g/5 oz chestnut mushrooms, small ones left whole, larger ones halved or quartered
100 g/3½ oz oyster mushrooms, larger ones cut into pieces
Salt to taste
Slivers of fresh red chillies, to garnish

For the special garam masala
10 black peppercorns
½ tsp coriander seeds
1 clove
1 green cardamom pod
1 small sliver of cinnamon stick
1 pinch mustard seeds
1 pinch cumin seeds

Dry-roast the spices for the garam masala over a medium heat for about 1 minute, being careful they do not burn, then grind them together into a powder.

Heat the oil in a pan and fry the onion until translucent. Add the green chillies, ginger and garlic and allow them to soften, then add the powdered spices, turmeric and vinegar. Stir well and add the coriander leaves and the water. Simmer for 5 minutes.

Purée the mixture in a blender or food processor and return to the stove. Put in the mushrooms and simmer until they are tender, about 5 minutes. Add salt to taste and serve hot, garnished with slivers of fresh red chillies.

Chef Sundeep Bhagat is our pundit of vegetarian cuisine. He has a special flair for wedding banquets. Mild yet rich-tasting, this dish with its spicy tomato sauce may change the way you think about potatoes!

stuffed potatoes in sauce
ALOO DUM

SERVES 4

500 g/1 lb 2 oz medium potatoes, preferably red-skinned
Vegetable oil, to deep-fry
60 g/2 oz paneer
1 tbsp raisins
1 tsp fresh coriander leaves, chopped
Salt to taste
4 tbsp vegetable oil
1 tsp peeled and finely chopped fresh ginger
½ tsp cumin seeds
½ fresh red chilli, chopped
½ tsp turmeric powder
1 tbsp cornflour
2 cloves
1.5 cm/½ in length cinnamon
150 g/5 oz Spanish onion, chopped
1 garlic clove, peeled and chopped
½ tsp paprika powder
½ tsp coriander powder
½ tsp garam masala powder (see page 19)
250 g/9 oz tomatoes, chopped
300 ml/½ pint water
60 g/2 oz ground almonds
2 tbsp fresh cream
Almond slivers and a swirl of cream, to garnish

Boil the potatoes, whole and unpeeled, in salted water until cooked right through, about 25 minutes. Allow to cool, then peel and halve them. Heat the deep-frying oil to 180°C/350°F and deep-fry potato halves until they turn golden brown, about 2 minutes. Drain on absorbent kitchen paper and, when they have cooled, scoop the flesh out of the centres, set the shells aside and crumble the flesh. Grate the paneer and mix with half the crumbled potato flesh. Add the raisins, chopped coriander leaves and salt to taste.

Heat 1 tbsp oil in a pan and put in half the chopped ginger, cumin seeds, red chilli and turmeric powder and fry over medium heat for 1 minute. Add to the potato flesh and paneer and mix well. Fill the scooped out potato shells with the mixture and dust with cornflour.

Heat the remaining oil in a pan and put in the cloves, cinnamon and onion. Fry over a medium heat until the onion is translucent. Add the remainder of the ginger and the garlic and cook, stirring, for 3 minutes before adding the spice powders. Then add the tomatoes and simmer for 10 minutes before adding ⅓ of the water to moisten. Continue to simmer until the tomatoes are soft, about 10 minutes more.

Meanwhile add another ⅓ of the water to the ground almonds, make a paste and stir it in to the tomato mixture, adding salt to taste. If more liquid is needed, add the rest of the water and return briefly to the boil. Finally, blend or process the tomato mixture into a smooth sauce.

Re-heat the deep-frying oil and deep-fry the stuffed potatoes for 2 minutes while re-heating the sauce. Drain the potatoes, cut in half and place in a serving dish. Add the cream to the sauce and pour it over the potatoes. Garnish with almond slivers and a swirl of cream.

A spicy, tomato-rich sauce provides the perfect foil for

an unusual combination of vegetables, which should remain

crunchily *al dente*.

vegetables in kadai sauce
KADAI SUBZI

SERVES 4

2 tbsp vegetable oil
1 tsp cumin seeds
½ tsp onion seeds
1 tsp turmeric powder
1 tsp red chilli powder
90 g/3 oz broccoli, in small florets
90 g/3 oz cauliflower, in small florets
90 g/3 oz courgettes, sliced into thin roundels
90 g/3 oz carrots, sliced into thin roundels
90 g/3 oz French beans, cut into 2.5 cm/1 in lengths
90 g/3 oz baby corn, cut into 3 pieces
150 ml/5 fl oz Kadai sauce (see page 131)
1 knob butter
Fresh coriander and cherry tomatoes, to garnish
Salt to taste

Heat the oil in a pan and put in the cumin and onion seeds. When they pop, after about 30 seconds, lower heat and add the turmeric and red chilli powders. Add all the vegetables, increasing the heat again, and toss for 2 minutes. Add a little water, reduce the heat, and simmer for 3 minutes more, then add the Kadai sauce and cook until the vegetables are done, about 3 more minutes.

Stir in the knob of butter and serve garnished with fresh coriander and cherry tomatoes.

This dish is a creation of our Chef Ramesh Chand. The crisp roots are simply tossed in quickly fried onions and chillies. You can use canned lotus roots if you can't find any fresh ones.

crispy fried lotus root
KAMAL KARKI JAIPURI

SERVES 4

350 g/12 oz lotus roots, carefully washed,
   peeled and thinly sliced
Salt
1 tsp red chilli powder
1½ tsp turmeric powder
3 tbsp gram flour
3 tbsp cornflour
Vegetable oil, to deep-fry
2 tbsp vegetable oil, to pan-fry
2 red onions, chopped
1 green chilli, finely chopped
1 red chilli, finely chopped
½ tsp chaat masala
2 tsp lemon juice
3–4 stems fresh coriander, chopped
More fresh coriander and fresh red chillies
   cut into julienne (matchstick) strips, to garnish
Salt, for sprinkling

Dry the lotus slices on kitchen paper and sprinkle them with salt, red chilli and turmeric powders. Leave for 2–3 minutes, then dust with a mixture of the gram flour and cornflour.

Heat the deep-frying oil to 170°C/325°F and deep-fry the roots in batches until they are golden brown, about 1 to 2 minutes. Transfer to kitchen paper to soak up excess oil.

Heat 2 tbsp oil in a pan and put in the chopped red onions over high heat, adding the chillies after a few seconds. Toss for half a minute, then mix in the lotus root slices and remove from the heat. All the ingredients should be crisp and dry.

Sprinkle over the chaat masala, lemon juice, coriander and salt to taste. Serve hot with coriander and red chillies julienne as garnish.

This robust chickpea dish is given a special tang by the addition of sun-dried and powdered mango.

chickpeas and potatoes
PUNJABI CHOLE

SERVES 4

325g/11½ oz dried chickpeas
1 tsp bicarbonate of soda
4 cm/1¾ in length finger of fresh ginger, peeled and finely chopped
4–5 garlic cloves, peeled and finely chopped
3 tbsp vegetable oil
½ tsp cumin seeds
2 medium Spanish onions, chopped
2 green chillies, finely chopped
½ tsp red chilli powder
½ tsp coriander powder
½ tsp cumin powder
½ tsp paprika powder
150 g/5 oz tomatoes, peeled and chopped
2 tbsp tomato purée
60 g/2 oz baby new potatoes
4 tsp chana masala powder
2 tsp dried mango powder
Salt to taste
½ a lime
Fresh coriander and red chillies sliced into julienne (matchstick) strips, to garnish

Soak the chickpeas in water with the bicarbonate of soda overnight. The following day, drain and cover them with fresh cold water. Bring to the boil and cook over medium heat until tender, about 45 minutes. Drain and set aside.

Pound or process the ginger and garlic together with a little water to make a paste. Heat the oil in a pan. Add the cumin seeds and cook for a few seconds until they pop, then put in the chopped onion and sauté until brown. Add the ginger and garlic paste and the green chillies and continue to sauté until the paste too is light brown, then lower the heat and add the powdered chilli, coriander, cumin and paprika. Stir-fry for 1 minute, add the tomatoes and cook over medium heat for 20 minutes to reduce. Add the tomato purée and simmer for 2 to 3 minutes.

Meanwhile, in another pan boil the baby potatoes and halve them. Set aside.

Add the chickpeas and the chana masala to the tomato mixture and simmer over low heat for a further 15 to 20 minutes. Add the mango powder and salt to taste, stir in the boiled baby potatoes and squeeze the lime juice over. Serve garnished with the coriander and red chillies.

A typical vegetable stew, served at

Parsee weddings.

parsee
vegetable stew
LAGANSHALA

SERVES 4

4 tbsp vegetable oil
75 g/2¾ oz green peas
Vegetable oil, to deep-fry
75 g/2¾ oz French beans, cut into 1 cm/¼ in lengths
75 g/2¾ oz cauliflower, cut into very small florets
1 carrot, peeled and extremely finely diced
1 medium potato, peeled and extremely finely diced
1 sweet potato, peeled and extremely finely diced
75 g/2¾ oz yam, peeled and extremely finely diced
5 cm/2 in length of ginger, peeled and finely chopped
4–6 garlic cloves, peeled and finely chopped
4–5 whole dried red chillies
3 Spanish onions, finely chopped
3–4 fresh green chillies, finely chopped
1 tsp cumin powder
3 tomatoes, chopped
3 tbsp malt vinegar
2 tbsp sugar
Salt to taste
A few stems of fresh coriander and fresh mint, chopped,
    and halved cherry tomatoes (optional) to garnish

Heat 1 tbsp of the vegetable oil in a pan and briefly sauté the green peas, about 1 minute. Drain and set aside.

Heat the deep-frying oil to 180°C/350°F and deep-fry the vegetables, each variety separately, for 1 to 2 minutes. Drain on absorbent paper.

Crush the ginger, garlic and dried red chillies together with a little water in a mortar or process to a paste.

Heat the remaining 3 tbsp of oil in a pan and brown the chopped onions. Add the ginger, garlic and dried red chilli paste and the green chillies and cook for 1 to 2 minutes. Add the cumin powder and the tomatoes and cook until the tomatoes are reduced to a pulpy consistency, about 8 to 10 minutes. Add the vinegar, sugar and salt, stir and toss in the vegetables. Mix well and cook for a further 3 to 4 minutes. Serve scattered with the coriander and mint and garnished, if you like, with halved cherry tomatoes.

RICE AND BREAD

plain white basmati rice
SAFED CHAWAL

SERVES 4

500 g/1 lb 2 oz Basmati rice
3 litres/5¼ pints water
2 tsp salt

Wash the rice in running water, soak for one hour and drain. Bring the water to the boil in a large pan, add the salt and then the rice. Cook uncovered over medium heat until the rice is just done, about 15 minutes. Drain and serve hot.

saffron rice
KESARIA PILAU

SERVES 4

500 g/1lb 2 oz Basmati rice
3 tbsp vegetable ghee
4 cloves
4 green cardamom pods
2.5 cm/1 in length cinnamon stick
1 bay leaf
½ medium Spanish onion, chopped
1.25 litres/2½ pints water
½ tsp saffron strands
Salt to taste
A sprinkling of almond flakes and sultanas, to garnish

Wash the rice under running water and soak for 1 hour. Drain.

Pre-heat the oven to 130°C/250°F/Gas Mark ½.*

Heat the ghee on top of the stove in a casserole dish. Add the whole spices and the bay leaf, followed after a few seconds by the chopped onion. Fry over medium heat until the onion is translucent, then add the water, saffron strands and salt and bring to the boil.

Add the rice and return to the boil. Lower the flame and allow the rice to boil gently, uncovered, until enough water has evaporated to bring it to the level of the rice, when bubbles will be visible on the surface, 5 to 6 minutes.

Stir the rice once, put the lid on the casserole dish and transfer to the oven for a further 10 to 12 minutes.

Serve hot, garnished with the almond flakes and sultanas.

* The very low heat required to allow the rice to absorb the liquid slowly is best achieved by finishing it in a covered pan in a low oven. You can, however, simply cover the pan and cook for 15 minutes on top of the stove with the heat source reduced to a minimum.

The addition of wild rice and cashew nuts
to this unique Porte des Indes recipe imparts
a very special flavour.

coconut rice
RIZ AU COCO

SERVES 4

100 g/3½ oz wild rice
400 g/14 oz Basmati rice
150 g/5 oz butter
1 tsp sesame seeds
2 tbsp raisins
2 tbsp whole cashew nuts
200 g/7 oz desiccated coconut
3 tbsp sugar
Salt to taste
Fried curry leaves, to garnish

First cook both types of rice. Cook the wild rice separately from the Basmati, following the instructions on the packet. (It will probably take longer than the plain Basmati rice, which should be cooked by the method described opposite.)

Meanwhile, in another pan, melt the butter, add the sesame seeds, then the raisins and cashew nuts and fry briefly over a medium heat until the nuts begin to turn light brown. Lower the heat, add the desiccated coconut and continue to fry very gently, stirring continuously until the coconut begins to brown, about 1 minute. Mix in the sugar and salt to taste and remove the pan from the heat.

Add the two boiled rices and toss lightly to mix, taking care not to break the grains. Serve hot, garnished with fried curry leaves.

This Southern Indian recipe is very popular served with natural yoghurt and spicy lime or mango pickle. Channa dal is widely available either under that name or as Bengal gram.

lime rice
YELEMECAM SADAM

SERVES 4

500 g/1lb 2 oz Basmati rice
2 tbsp vegetable oil
1 level tsp mustard seeds
1 tbsp channa dal
½ Spanish onion, sliced
1 fresh green chilli, chopped into julienne
   (fine matchstick) strips
1 sprig curry leaves
½ tsp turmeric powder
1.25 litres/2½ pints water
Juice of 4 limes
Salt to taste
Chopped fresh coriander and lime wedges, to garnish

Wash the rice under running water and soak it for 1 hour. Drain.

Pre-heat the oven to 130°C/250°F/Gas Mark ½.

Heat the vegetable oil in a casserole on top of the stove and drop in the mustard seeds and channa dal. As soon as the mustard seeds pop and the dal begins to turn brown, add the onion, chillies and the curry leaves. Fry until the onion is translucent, then add the turmeric powder.

Pour in the water, bring to the boil, and add the lime juice and salt. Mix in the drained rice, return the mixture to the boil, lower the heat a little and boil steadily until enough of the water has evaporated to lower it to the level of the rice, about 5 minutes.

Cover the pan with a tight-fitting lid and transfer to the oven for 10 to 12 minutes. Serve hot, garnished with the fresh coriander and lime wedges.

To make this traditional accompaniment to Kerala red fish curry you will need a semolina press. Made of aluminium and available cheaply in Indian stores, it's a cylindrical container with a plunger at one end and a selection of perforated discs to be placed at the other end. To make stringhoppers you need to use the disc with the finest perforations. You can also use this press to make your own noodles. A more expensive version comes in brass and makes an unusual decorative object for your kitchen!

stringhoppers
IDIAPPAM

MAKES 6 PORTIONS

125 ml/4 fl oz water
½ tbsp vegetable oil
Salt to taste
180 g/6 oz roasted red rice flour
   (available at Indian grocers)
60 g/2 oz fresh coconut, grated

Bring the water to the boil. Add the vegetable oil and a little salt and remove from the heat.

Put the rice flour in a mixing bowl and slowly add the hot water, stirring constantly to prevent lumps forming. Knead well to make a soft dough.

Divide the dough into about 6 portions and press each in turn through the semolina press on to the tray of a steamer.

Steam for 7 to 10 minutes, transfer to plates, sprinkle freshly grated coconut over and serve hot.

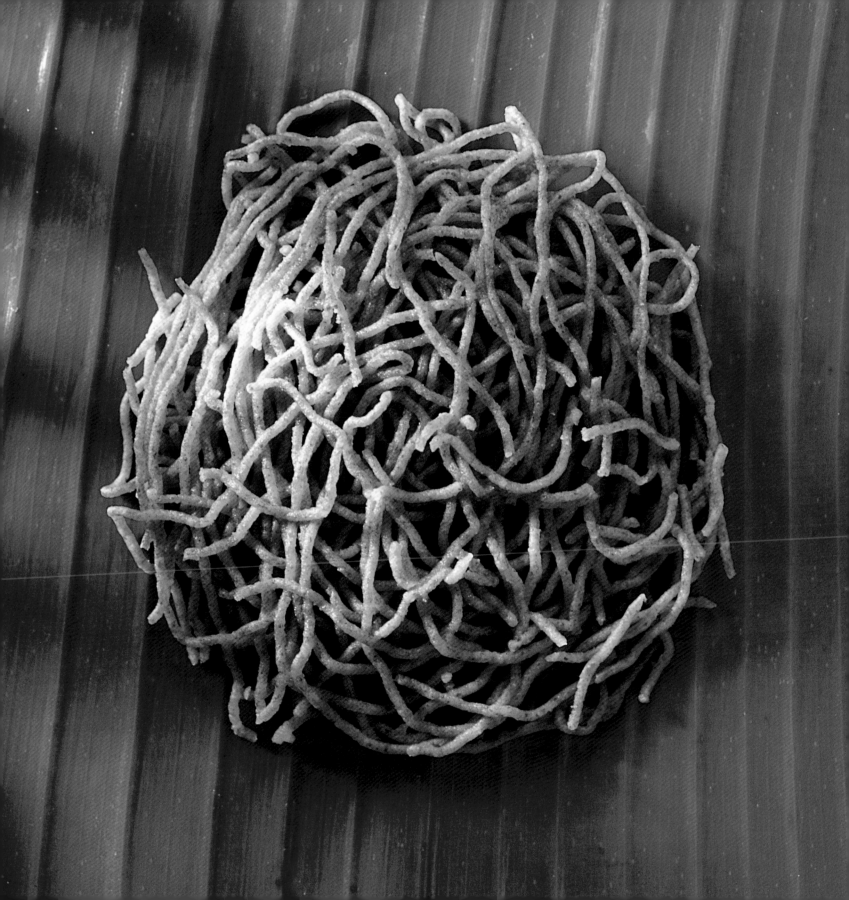

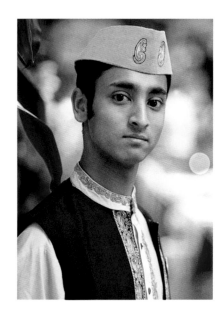

An unusual rice flour pancake, a speciality of Pondicherry where it's called *appams*. Like any pancake, Pain Créole should be eaten immediately, while it's hot.

rice pancakes
PAIN CRÉOLE

MAKES 8

1 tbsp boiled Basmati rice (see page 120)
100 ml/3½ fl oz water
250 g/8½ oz rice flour
500 ml/17 fl oz coconut milk
1 tsp sugar
1 pinch dry yeast
1 pinch salt
A little vegetable oil, to cook

Make a paste with the cooked rice and the water and mix in all the remaining ingredients except the vegetable oil. Set the mixture aside in a warm place for 3 hours.

Oil a small frying pan or omelette pan, about 15 cm/6 in diameter, which you can cover with a lid. Heat over a medium heat, pour in a ladleful of the mixture, tilting and swirling the pan so that it covers the base, as though you were making a pancake. Return the pan to the heat, cover with the lid and cook for about 2 minutes until the edges of the mixture turn light brown, then ease the cooked Pain Créole out of the pan.

This tandoori-baked bread, with its satisfying texture that combines scorched crust and soft crumb, and its long oval shape that invites tearing, is simple to prepare and to bake in a conventional oven. Serve it hot from the oven with any grill.

naan bread

TO SERVE 4–6

250 g/9 oz plain white flour
1 pinch of salt
½ tsp bicarbonate of soda
1 tbsp yoghurt, preferably Greek
125 ml/4 fl oz whole milk
1 tbsp sugar
½ egg, beaten
1½ tbsp vegetable oil

Put the flour, salt and bicarbonate of soda in a bowl and mix well. In another bowl, whisk the yoghurt, milk, sugar and egg together and then stir this mixture into the flour mixture to form a soft dough. Place the dough on a flat, lightly floured surface and knead for 3 minutes.

Add the vegetable oil and knead for a further 2 minutes. Then cover with cling film and set aside.

Preheat oven to 240°C/475°F/Gas Mark 9.

Divide the dough into 16 portions. Flatten each one with your hand and stretch into a tear-drop shape. Alternatively roll them into ovals with a rolling pin. The flattened dough should be about 5 mm/¼ in thick.

Cook in the oven for 5–7 minutes (or against the side walls of a tandoor oven for 2 minutes) until the naan is scorched brown in patches on the outside and soft and fluffy on the inside. Serve hot from the oven.

SAUCES AND CHUTNEYS

mango sauce

Pictured left, this sauce will keep for one week in the refrigerator or for three months in the freezer if frozen the day it is made.

MAKES 300 ML/½ PINT

1 green mango, peeled and cut into dice about 5 mm/¼ in thick
10 black peppercorns
1.5 cm/½ in length cinnamon stick
2.5 cm/1 in length finger of ginger, peeled and roughly chopped
4 cloves
1 bayleaf
100 g/3½ oz sugar
½ tsp turmeric powder
½ tsp salt
400 ml/14 fl oz water for a thick sauce (you may add more water if a thinner sauce is desired)

Place all the ingredients in a saucepan, bring to the boil and simmer for 20 to 30 minutes.

Allow to cool, push through a sieve and use as required.

kadai sauce

This sauce will keep for one week in the refrigerator or for one month in the freezer if it is allowed to cool and is frozen the day it is made.

MAKES 250 G/8½ OZ

6–7 whole black peppercorns
1½ tbsp coriander seeds
4–5 dried red chillies, seeds removed
3 tbsp vegetable oil
1 medium Spanish onion, chopped
3–4 garlic cloves, peeled and finely chopped
4 cm/1¾ in length finger of ginger, peeled and finely chopped
2 green chillies, chopped
½ tsp chilli powder
1 tsp paprika powder
300 g/10 oz tomatoes, finely chopped
1 tbsp tomato purée
Salt to taste

Lightly dry-roast the peppercorns, coriander seeds and dried red chillies in a frying pan for about 30 seconds, then lightly crush them in a mortar.

Heat the oil in a pan and cook the onion gently until translucent. Add the garlic and ginger and lightly brown. Increasing the heat, add the green chillies and sauté for 1 minute, then lower the heat again and add the roasted spices and the chilli and paprika powders.

After 1 minute add the chopped tomatoes and cook over medium heat until the mixture reduces by half, about 30 to 45 minutes. Stir in the tomato purée and season with salt to taste.

mint sauce

TO MAKE 500 ML/18 FL OZ

1 small bunch mint, stalks removed
1 small bunch coriander, stalks removed
1 fresh green chilli
3–4 garlic cloves, peeled
1 tsp lemon juice
600 ml/1 pint plain yoghurt
1 tsp sugar, or to taste
½ tsp salt, or to taste

Blend or process the mint and coriander leaves, the chilli and the garlic into a fine paste with the lemon juice and a little water. Mix the paste into the yoghurt and whisk until a smooth sauce is obtained. Add the sugar and salt, chill and serve immediately, or within 3 to 4 days.

onion sauce

MAKES 700 ML/1¼ PINTS

6 tbsp vegetable oil
2 bay leaves
4 cloves
2.5 cm/1 in length cinnamon stick
1 black cardamom pod
1 kg/2 lb 2 oz Spanish onions, sliced
150 ml/5 fl oz water

Heat the oil in a pan, add the bay leaves and spices followed by the sliced onions and cook gently until the onions are translucent.

Add the water and bring to the boil. Simmer the onions to a pulp, about 30 minutes. Leave to cool, then purée the sauce. Store in the refrigerator for up to a week or in the freezer for up to a month, using as required.

tamarind sauce

TO MAKE 500ML/18 FL OZ

200 g/7 oz tamarind block
1.5 litres/2½ pints water
2.5 cm/1 in length cinnamon stick
2.5 cm/1 in length finger of ginger, peeled and roughly chopped
1 bay leaf
1 tsp paprika powder
1 tsp cumin powder
300 g/10 oz jaggery
Salt to taste

Soak the tamarind block in a pan in 1 litre/1¾ pints water for 10 minutes. Add the cinnamon, ginger and bay leaf, bring to the boil and simmer for 30 minutes. Allow to cool, then pour through a sieve set over a bowl, pressing down with a pestle or the underside of a ladle to extract as much liquid as possible from the solids in the sieve.

Soak the residual tamarind pulp in the remaining 500 ml/ 17 fl oz water for 15 to 20 minutes and sieve again, then stir it into the mixture.

Add the paprika and cumin powders, the jaggery and salt to taste and simmer for a further 15 minutes. Allow to cool, then use as required. The sauce will keep for 1 week in the refrigerator or up to 3 months in the deep-freeze.

karwari coconut chutney

This sauce may be kept in the refrigerator for up to a week or in the freezer for a month if frozen the same day.

MAKES 350 G/12 OZ

30 g/1 oz dried tamarind pulp
4–5 dried red chillies
150 g/5 oz fresh coconut, grated*
4 garlic cloves, peeled and roughly chopped
3 shallots, peeled and roughly chopped
3 tsp paprika powder
½ tsp turmeric powder
Salt to taste
2 tbsp vegetable oil
½ tsp mustard seeds
1 stem curry leaves

Soak the dried tamarind pulp in hot water for 10–15 minutes to soften. Seed the dried red chillies unless you want your chutney to be very spicy.

Process together the grated coconut, garlic, shallots and dried chillies, moistening with a little water. Mix in the softened tamarind pulp and add the paprika and turmeric powders and salt to taste.

Heat the oil in a pan, put in the mustard seeds and, when they splutter after a few seconds, add the curry leaves and pour over the processed mixture, mixing well.

We only use fresh coconut. Chop the coconut in two with a cleaver and remove the flesh by sliding a sharp knife between it and the hard shell. This may seem a great deal of trouble to prepare one dish, but you can make a larger quantity of chutney and freeze the rest.

créole sauce

This sauce will keep for one week in the refrigerator or for one month in the freezer if frozen the same day.

MAKES 500 ML/17 FL OZ

500 g/1 lb 2 oz tomatoes, cut in half and base of stem removed
100 g/3½ oz white radish, roughly chopped
100g/3½ oz red bell pepper, roughly sliced
1 fresh red chilli, roughly chopped
1 tsp onion seeds
2 tbsp sultanas
½ tsp paprika powder
½ tsp garam masala powder
2 tbsp tomato purée
2–3 tbsp sugar
4 tsp malt vinegar
Salt to taste

Put the halved tomatoes, radish, bell pepper and red chillies in a pan with water to cover and boil over medium heat to reduce, 30 to 45 minutes. Remove from the heat and blend.

Strain and discard residue. Add the onion seeds, sultanas, paprika and garam masala powders, tomato purée and sugar. Simmer to further reduce until a sauce consistency is obtained, about 10-15 minutes.

Stir in the vinegar, add salt to taste and allow to cool.

smoked tomato chutney
TOMATO ROUGAIL

At La Porte des Indes this typically Créole spicy tomato sauce is served with grilled lobster. Try it also with prawns and other fish. It will keep for a week in the refrigerator or a month in the freezer.

MAKES 650 ML/22 FL OZ

4 tbsp vegetable oil
1 tsp mustard seeds
1 red onion, chopped
6–7 garlic cloves, finely sliced
2 stems curry leaves
3 green chillies, chopped
1 kg/2 lb 3 oz tomatoes, chopped
1 tbsp paprika powder
1 tsp chilli powder
1 tsp coriander powder
2 tbsp tomato purée
1½ tbsp sugar
Salt to taste

Heat the oil in a pan, put in the mustard seeds and when they splutter after a few seconds add the red onion, garlic and curry leaves and cook until the onion is translucent, about 2 minutes. Add the chillies and sauté for 1 minute.

Add the chopped tomatoes. Bring to the boil and cook over medium heat until the mixture is reduced by half, about 20 minutes. Add the paprika, chilli and coriander powders and the tomato purée. Cook for 2 to 3 minutes more, adding the sugar and salt to taste.

yoghurt dip
RAITA

The deliciously simple, universal cooling accompaniment to any Indian meal.

SERVES 4

1 tsp cumin seeds, dry roasted and ground into a powder
½ tsp red chilli powder
½ tsp paprika powder
1 pinch sugar
200 ml/7 fl oz natural yoghurt
60 g/2 oz cucumber, unpeeled, seeded and cut into the finest possible dice
1 red onion, cut into very fine dice
1 medium tomato, seeded and cut into the finest possible dice

Whisk the spices and the sugar into the yoghurt, then stir in the remaining ingredients and serve chilled.

(You can improvise your own vegetable raita using, for example, spinach, briefly blanched and shredded, or shredded carrot. Or make a sweet raita with fruits, e.g. apples, bananas or pineapple.)

DESSERTS

Star anise adds an exotic note to this exceptionally light version of a classic chocolate mousse.

star anise chocolate mousse

SERVES 6

4 egg yolks
30 g/1 oz caster sugar
200 g/7 oz finest quality dark chocolate
60 g/2 oz butter
1½ tsp star anise powder
6 egg whites
15 g/½ oz white chocolate
1 tbsp double cream

Whip the egg yolks and half the sugar together in a mixing bowl until it holds a ribbon when you lift some on the beaters and trail it back into the bulk of the mixture. Melt the dark chocolate and half the butter in a *bain marie* (double boiler) to make a smooth emulsion. Add the star anise powder and fold into the yolk mixture.

In another bowl whip the egg whites, adding the remaining sugar when the whites are still floppy but just beginning to form soft peaks, then continue beating until the mixture holds stiff peaks. Set aside 2 tbsp of the whites mixture and fold the dark chocolate mixture very gently into the rest, being careful to retain as much air as possible.

Melt the white chocolate with the remainder of the butter, add the cream and fold into the remaining 2 tbsp of egg whites. Divide the dark chocolate mousse between 6 ramekins or glasses. Top with the white chocolate mousse, working it into a star design if you wish.

Rose petals to be eaten should come from flowers grown without pesticides or other garden chemicals, which rules out most shop-bought roses. Rose syrup can be found in Indian stores and many supermarkets now stock it.

rose-flavoured milk and ground rice pudding
RIZ AU LAIT AU CONFIT DE ROSES

SERVES 8

5 tbsp Basmati rice
1 litre/1¾ pints full-cream fresh milk
5 tbsp sugar
2 tbsp rose syrup
60 g/2 oz *confit de roses* (or rose jelly or jam)
100 ml/3½ fl oz double cream
Edible rose petals, to decorate

Wash and soak the rice in cold water for 8 to 10 minutes. Drain and grind the rice finely in a grinder or food processor. Alternatively, use ready-ground rice, adding a little water to make a paste.

Bring the milk to boiling point in a pan and stir in the sugar and then the ground rice paste. Simmer the mixture until it thickens, then add the rose syrup, *confit de roses* and double cream. Pour into 8 small moulds, allow to cool and refrigerate. Serve the pudding in the moulds, decorated with the rose petals.

This delicious dessert was created by our Chef Asif, affectionately known as "Halwai", who is a seventh generation sweet maker from Jhellum in Rawalpindi.

apple malpua

SERVES 6

2 apples, preferably Golden Delicious or Granny Smith
Juice of 1/2 lemon
Oil to depth in frying pan of about 1.5 cm/1/2 in
4 tbsp icing sugar
1 tsp cinnamon powder
Cinnamon or vanilla ice cream, to serve

For the batter:
100 g/3 1/2 oz plain flour
100 g/3 1/2 oz rice flour
8 tsp semolina
200 ml/7 fl oz single cream

For the syrup:
250 g/9 oz sugar
500 ml/18 fl oz water
2.5 cm/1 in length cinnamon stick
1 slice of lemon

First make the batter by mixing all the batter ingredients together and adding a little water to achieve a thick, coating consistency. Allow to rest for 2 hours in a warm place.

Peel, core and slice the apples very thinly. Set aside in a bowl of cold water with the juice of 1/2 lemon squeezed into it.

For the syrup, dissolve the sugar in the water over heat, add the cinnamon and lemon and boil until the syrup reduces to a sticky consistency. Remove the slice of lemon.

When the batter has rested, heat the oil to 180°C/360°F, dip the apple slices into the batter in batches, dropping them immediately into the hot oil. Let them brown on one side for 2 minutes then turn to brown on the other side for a further 2 minutes. Remove from the oil and dip into the hot (but not boiling) syrup for 30 seconds. Arrange the apple slices on a serving dish and sprinkle over the icing sugar and cinnamon powder mixed together. Serve with cinnamon or vanilla ice cream.

Chickoos (also known as sapodilla) are a uniquely delicious fruit, well worth searching for. If you can't find them fresh they can be obtained in cans at Chinese supermarkets.

chickoo halwaa

SERVES 6

150 g/5 oz chickoos
150 g/5 oz butter
150 g/5 oz semolina
200 g/7 oz sugar
Slivered almonds, to decorate

Peel, stone, chop and purée the chickoos. Melt the butter in a pan and fry the semolina until it turns a golden brown.

Heat 500 ml/18 fl oz of water and dissolve the sugar in it, then boil to a temperature of 105°C/220°F to reduce to a syrup that will pour off a spoon in a single thread. Allow to cool, then add the chickoo purée.

Over medium heat, slowly add the mixture to the semolina, stirring constantly, and cook until it leaves the sides of the pan. Serve hot, in individual bowls decorated with slivered almonds.

This stunning variation on kulfi (Indian ice cream) is an original

Porte des Indes creation.

belgian chocolate and praline ice cream

CHOCOLATE AND CHIKKI KULFI

SERVES 6

150 g/5 oz sugar
1 tbsp liquid glucose
75 g/2½ oz cashew nuts
750 ml/1¼ pints full-cream milk
300 ml/½ pint double cream
25 g/1 oz white chocolate
200 g/7 oz best quality dark chocolate
White chocolate flakes, to decorate (optional).

Dissolve 100 g/3½ oz sugar in enough water to cover, add the glucose and cook to a light caramel.

Roast the cashew nuts in a medium-hot oven until they are light brown and add to the caramel. Spread the mixture on a lightly oiled baking tray and, when it has cooled and set into a praline, crush it into very small pieces and set aside, or store in an air-tight tin if you make it in advance.

Boil the milk until it is reduced by half, about 25 minutes. Add the remaining sugar and simmer for a few more minutes until it has the consistency of a cream sauce. Add the cream, bring back to the boil and simmer for 10 minutes over very low heat, then add the white chocolate and whisk vigorously.

Melt the dark chocolate in a double boiler or a microwave oven and immediately stir into the mixture. Allow to partially cool and add the praline bits.

Transfer the mixture to a freezer container and allow to cool, then place it in the freezer and leave for about an hour until it is firm round the edges. Beat the mixture, return to the freezer and beat twice more at hourly intervals, until you have achieved a creamy consistency. (Alternatively, if you have an ice cream maker, follow the manufacturer's instructions.)

Transfer the ice cream from freezer to fridge 20 to 30 minutes before serving. To serve, scoop into individual chilled bowls and sprinkle, if you like, with white chocolate flakes.

Palm syrup is integral to the flavour of this dish and can be found in Chinese supermarkets. Try to obtain fresh green coconuts as the flesh is more tender than the hard brown type.

green lentils and tender coconut pudding
PAYASAM

SERVES 8

200 g/7 oz moong dal
8 tbsp vegetable ghee
250 g/8 oz palm syrup
100 g/3½ oz sugar
250 ml/9 fl oz coconut cream
5 tbsp double cream
15 g/½ oz cashew nuts
15 g/½ oz sultanas
150 g/5 oz tender green coconut, sliced

Fry the moong dal brown in 6 tbsp ghee. Add 800 ml/27 fl oz water, bring to the boil and gently simmer for 30 minutes. Add the palm syrup and continue to simmer until the dal are fully cooked – about 15 minutes.

Add the sugar, coconut cream and double cream and simmer for a further 10 minutes. Meanwhile heat the remaining ghee and fry the cashew nuts and sultanas. Add to the lentil mixture with the slices of tender coconut and serve piping hot.

Red rice imparts a mildly nutty flavour to this unusual dessert. An original creation, it was inspired by Mehernosh Mody's travels in the backwaters of Kerala.

red rice *crème brûlée* with jackfruit

SERVES 6

250 ml/8 fl oz milk
30 g/1 oz red rice, washed and drained
3 egg yolks
60 g/2 oz sugar
400 ml/14 fl oz double cream, chilled
Pinch of salt
½ tsp cinnamon powder
180 g/6 oz jackfruit, seeded and cut into thin strips
Dusting of icing sugar

Bring the milk to a boil. Add rice and cook until the grains are soft enough to be easily crushed by the back of a wooden spoon, about 25–30 minutes. Leave to cool to room temperature.

Preheat the oven to 175°C/350°F/Gas Mark 4.

Beat together the egg yolks and sugar. In a pan bring the double cream to a boil and add the rice mixture. Slowly add this mixture into the egg and sugar emulsion, a little at a time. Add the salt and cinnamon powder, mix well.

Spoon into ramekins, place the ramekins in a *bain marie* and bake in the oven for 15–20 minutes. When cooked, remove and place in the refrigerator to chill.

Top with the fanned out strips of jackfruit, dust with icing sugar and caramelise it under the grill or with a kitchen blowtorch. Allow the caramelised sugar to cool before serving.

COCKTAILS

The Porte des Indes' bar conjures up the atmosphere of a hunters' perch with its hurricane lamps, cane furniture, palm trees and, most of all, its panoramic paintings of animals in the jungle, the work of Rajasthani painter Dharindr from Jaipur. Following a tradition of colonial days at the Long Bar at Raffles Hotel in Singapore, drinkers are encouraged to throw their empty peanut shells on the floor as a humorous gesture of devil-may-care.

You can re-create a little of the atmosphere of this wittily romantic environment with some of these exotic cocktails.

Quantities in the following recipes are to make one drink.

monsoon

2 tbsp Midori
1 tbsp Skyy melon vodka
Champagne, to top up
Slice of green melon, to garnish

Shake the Midori and melon vodka together with ice. Pour into a champagne glass and top up with champagne. Garnish with a slice of green melon (pictured right).

coco passion

4–5 pieces diced pineapple
8–10 fresh basil leaves
Wedge of lime
1 tbsp sugar syrup
2 tbsp passion fruit juice or pulp
2½ tbsp Skyy vodka
1 tbsp Skyy citrus
⅓ of the water from a coconut (approx. 4–5 tbsp)
Ice, for shaking

Crush the pineapple, basil leaves and wedge of lime together. Add all the other ingredients, shake with ice and strain into a coconut shell. Garnish with a slice of passion fruit and more basil leaves (pictured above).

pondi cheri mon amour

1½ tbsp Angostura dark rum
1 tbsp vanilla liqueur
4–5 pieces pineapple, diced
⅓ of the water from a coconut (approx. 4–5 tbsp)
Orchid, to decorate

Blend all the ingredients together with ice in a shaker and pour into a coconut shell. Decorate with an orchid.

rose-e-tini

3–4 fresh lychees, stoned
2½ tbsp Plymouth gin
1½ tbsp rose liqueur
Rose petals, to decorate

Crush the lychees, mingle with the other ingredients, shake with ice and strain into a martini glass. Decorate with rose petals.

liquid gold

2½ tbsp Angostura dark rum
1½ tbsp double cream
2½ tbsp apple juice
1 medium chickoo fruit (sapodilla)*, puréed, plus 1 slice, to decorate

Shake all the ingredients together with ice and strain into a highball glass. Garnish with a slice of chickoo fruit.

*Chickoo fruit (sapodilla) has a brown skin and looks rather like a very large kiwi fruit. Sometimes available fresh, it can also be obtained canned in Chinese supermarkets.

indian cosmopolitan

2½ tbsp Tequila
1½ tbsp Grand Marnier
4 tbsp white cranberry juice
1 cm/½ inch piece ginger, crushed
Dash of lime juice
Dash of sugar syrup
Slice of ginger and a white orchid, to decorate

Shake all ingredients with ice and strain into a cocktail glass.
Garnish with a slice of ginger and a white orchid.

kama sutra

2½ tbsp Black vodka
2 tbsp Passoa
5 tbsp cranberry juice
Slice of star fruit, to decorate

Pour the cranberry juice and Passoa into a glass over crushed
ice. Pour the Black vodka slowly over the back of a spoon
held close to the inner rim of the glass, to form a separate
floating layer. Garnish with a slice of star fruit and sip the
cranberry juice and Passoa through the vodka (pictured left).

red dragon

3 strawberries
2 tbsp Skyy vodka
1 tbsp strawberry liqueur
1 tbsp vanilla liqueur
Ginger ale, for topping up
1 wedge of dragon fruit, to garnish

Blend all ingredients with ice in a blender, pour into a cocktail
glass, add ice cubes and top up with ginger ale. Garnish with
a slice of dragon fruit (pictured above).

tamarind martini

2½ tbsp Plymouth Gin
1 dash Limoncello
2 tbsp tamarind purée
Star fruit and a red chilli, to decorate

Shake all ingredients with ice and strain into a martini glass.
Decorate with star fruit and a red chilli.

french connection

2 tbsp Cherry Marnier
1 tbsp vanilla liqueur
Champagne, to top up
Fresh cherry or strawberry, to garnish

Shake the Cherry Marnier and vanilla liqueur together with ice.
Pour into a champagne glass and top up with champagne.
Garnish with a fresh cherry or a strawberry.

KEY TO SYMBOLS

spicy

medium spicy

very spicy

ACKNOWLEDGEMENTS

The Blue Elephant Group would like to extend their gratitude
to all those who contributed to this book's publication.
Special thanks go to Pat Chapman of the Good Curry Guide
for his continued support, L' Association des Comptoirs de l'Inde,
Paris, Les Grande Dames de Pondichery, The Romain Rolland
Library (earlier known as 'Bibliotheque Publique'), the Pondicherry
Museum, the Alliance Française and the French Institute who are
dedicated to keeping the French tradition alive in Pondicherry.
And last but not least, the staff of La Porte des Indes, for their
endless enthusiasm and team spirit.

First published in the United Kingdom in 2005 by PAVILION BOOKS

An imprint of Chrysalis Books Group plc

The Chrysalis Building, Bramley Road, London W10 6SP
www.chrysalisbooks.co.uk

Text © The Blue Elephant International plc, 2005
Photography © Tony le Duc, 2005
Photographs on pages 9 and 10 © La Porte des Indes
The photograph on page 4 is published with the kind permission of Pat Chapman
Design and layout © Pavilion Books, 2005

COMMISSIONING EDITOR Stuart Cooper
DESIGNER Isobel Gillan
PHOTOGRAPHER Tony le Duc
FOOD STYLIST Mehernosh Mody
SENIOR EDITOR Emily Preece-Morrison
COPY EDITOR Rosemary Stark
PROOFREADER Rebecca Wilson
INDEXER Hilary Bird

Reproduction by Classicscan Pte Ltd., Singapore
Printed in China

10 9 8 7 6 5 4 3 2 1

LA PORTE DES INDES LONDON, 32 Bryanston Street, London W1H 7EG, United Kingdom, Tel: +44 20 7224 0055
LA PORTE DES INDES BRUSSELS, 455 Avenue Louise, 1050 Brussels, Belgium, Tel: +32 2 647 8651
A member of the Blue Elephant International Group
www.LaPorteDesIndes.com